13 Years of College

Ron Bullock

Contents

Preface

At the tender age of eight my mother shared with me a book of poems following one of my boredom rants. I can't explain the immediate connection that I felt for the words I read that day. Later I toyed with writing and constructing my very own poems. Learning a creative way of expressing my thoughts soon grew to be my therapy and way of releasing fears, anxiety, stress, social concerns, and most of all—my joy and happiness.

Sometime around 2016 I came up with the grandiose idea of writing a book. I had no idea of what I'd write about—I just had a burning desire to write a book.

During my journey to find a topic, I sought inspiration through reading. I read countless books, and wrote poems, short stories, and creative free form...only to come up empty handed. I rummaged through old pictures and notebooks, and ran across the journal that I kept for a significant part of my prison sentence.

Reading through the journal, I was forced to relive moments that helped to shape my character. Thumbing through the pages, I witnessed myself grow mentally, spiritually, and socially. After taking my self-led journey, there was no longer any questions of a topic. Unbeknownst to me, I had written myself an outline during the majority of my incarceration. With a topic, I still had a lingering question of my "why."

Why would I tell the story of my prison experience? Why would anyone be interested in what I did while incarcerated? Honestly,I didn't know the answer.

With my topic and in search of my why, I just wrote. I allowed myself to become vulnerable and embrace each emotion and feeling that aroused during my writing process. I found my why through being authentic and true to myself.

I would tell my story because I knew there was someone incarcerated who didn't have a clue of what to do with their prison sentence. There's also family members of these individuals who don't know exactly what to tell them. I hope that my why is as beneficial to others as this writing process has been for me.

Chapter 1

A RUDE AWAKENING

O h man, what a horrible nightmare! With the pillow over my head, "Are you eating breakfast?", penetrated my ears.

What the hell is going on? Why is everyone mingling around with their boxers on and thong flip-flops? What did I get myself into? As I make an earnest attempt to get out of this fake comfort zone, a paper rustled under my feet. I looked at it in total disbelief.

One count of first-degree murder; one count of armed robbery with a dangerous weapon. This paper held the answers to all my questions. My nightmare was live and in color.

"Ronald M. Bullock put your jumpsuit on and report to the gate," said a slim, brown-complexion fellow who appeared to be in his early twenties, through a partial smile.

"Was' up? Where am I goin?"

The officer replied, "You got first appearance."

I was ushered to a room with a small television, displaying a judge on its screen. When I noticed a video camera in the room, I knew it meant the judge could see me too. He read my charges aloud, confirming what I'd read moments earlier. And it was official. I couldn't get out because I had the lowest yet most impossible bond to liberate me! "No bond."

As I left the room after hearing my charges, I was discombobulated, and drained of all the energy I've ever possessed, my future depleted of any hope of seeing my twins born. On my journey back to my cell I asked the officer if I could be moved to a single cell! I heard guys yelling, as we walked.

"Udy, what the hell are you doing in here?"

"Udy, what's up man?"

Udy, try to get over here."

"Udy, come outside."

"Udy, I heard you got fucked up!"

The officer told me he had to talk to his sergeant to see if he could get me moved. As I entered cell F-102, the faces inside it were all a blur to me and the sounds a chorus of meaningless voices. Numbed by my new reality, I beelined to the place where the nightmare began and tried to sleep it off. The barrage of questions fell on deaf ears.

In confusion it's imperative to get some alone time and seek clarity. Lesson number one for me.

My message was relayed to the sergeant, and I was moved before his shift ended for the day. I was left alone with nothing but my thoughts to figure out my game plan. I knew I had to detach myself from the "free world" emotionally. That was the hardest part. Erasing every woman I cared about out from my existence was one hell of a task. I could no longer pursue futures with Isha, Angel, Denise, or ShiRon. It was a hell of a thing to accept.

My new living quarters were an eight by eight single cell, referred to as "the hole." The hole in most scenarios is used for punishment, but I used it as a tool to put everything into perspective. I needed to figure out the road ahead, dealing with the justice system, missing my family, and the unknown consequences of my poor decisions.

Bang, bang, bang!

"Ronald Bullock, get dressed. You have a visit," an NFL defensive end–sized white guy with a flat-top haircut demanded as he rapped on my door.

The jolt roused me from my pensive slumber. I wiped my face with a cold rag and stretched.

I lay waiting on my bed, hands clasped behind my head. The defensive end returned and opened the door to my cell, motioning for me with his head. I pulled on my orange jumpsuit slowly over my bare chest as I walked out of the room. With every step, my mind raced. Who had come to visit? Had my mother talked to my lawyer? Would I cry when I saw the pain etched on her face? The pain that I'd caused her?

How would I respond when I saw Angel crying while she carried a part of me inside her? Could I return my father's smile that was often a part of his facial features? As I strode down the white stale-smelling hallways, I forced my mind to empty itself of these emotional images. Entering the visitation room, I saw faces on bodies with orange jumpsuits—faces that were all a blur again having incomprehensible conversations. My eyes were locked in on faces that were on the other side of the long vertical plexiglass that separated the jumpsuit crew from the visitors on the other side. It was my parents and Angel. They all gave me dry, tired smiles, and I could tell I'd gotten more sleep than the three of them combined. Two days of incarceration and I could already notice the stress lines etched on my parents' brows.

Eyeing the holes drilled into the Plexiglass, I worried I wouldn't be able to hear my mother's monotone voice. When she spoke, however, I found I held onto every syllable as though my life depended on it.

"Baby, I want you to start talking to the Lord, 'cause if you did it or not you 'gone need him." She paused like she was gathering her thoughts and added, "Being a young black man in this town, we're up against a lot."

I dropped my head and covered my face, holding on to her words. When I looked up, my dad and Angel were nodding in agreement. Mom got up so that dad or Angel could talk; too emotionally drained, they both declined, so mom sat down again.

"Baby, once we leave we're going to head over to the lawyer's office. We need to see what he can do about getting you a bond." I tried to smile with her in that window of hope, but could see her bottom lip quivering just like mine. "Baby, I want you to start falling on your knees, talking to the Lord and reading your Bible."

"I will. I'm sure it ain't hard to find one in this place."

"More than anything I need you to keep your head up and find Jesus."

"I love ya'll," I said, wiping a lone tear.

The three of them replied in unison, knowing our time was limited, "I love you too."

And just like that, my visit was over. I stood and watched them file out a glass door. Just as the door closed, it swung back open and Angel re-entered alone.

"Udy, what am I going to do without you? I can't have these babies without you!"

"Baby, we are going to be alright. I promise you," I said to reassure her, but my words didn't convince me.

My dad returned to get her, and the officer unlocked the visitation door for me to leave. Back in the cell, I sat on my bunk. Head in my hands, I lost myself in my thoughts after all the excitement.

Lesson number two: your decisions not only affect you but also have a direct effect on those who love and care for you.

"Udy, what's up home boy?"

I couldn't make out the voice or the direction it came from. Wearing only my boxers, I slowly rolled out of my bunk, walked to the door, and replied in a halfhearted tone, "What's up?"

The voice echoed again, "You don't know who you talking to, do you?"

I really didn't. And couldn't care less about playing the guessing game. "Nah. Who is it?"

"Big OJ."

OJ was a big light-skinned old head I knew from the streets who kept his hands in a little of everything, from washing cars and cutting grass to selling a little drugs here and there. OJ was the type of guy who everyone in town knew and OJ knew everyone. His hustle depended on his social skills.

"Oh man, what's up Oj?"

"Yeah cu', I heard you talking to the C.O. when you came in from V.I. What you got going on cu?"

"I'm good. Just trying to figure this shit out."

"I dig it. Who came to see you? Ron and Tesi? What you in da hole for cu'?"

"Yeah. They brought my girl too. I came to get my head together for a while."

"Well, hurry the hell up and get your head together quick. This solitary shit gone' drive yo' ass crazy. Fuck around and you gone' be talking to these damn roaches. Just a tip from a G to a young G—let that girl go and focus, 'cause you facing some serious shit cu'. You can't fight these charges and worry about a damn girlfriend. How old are you cu?

"Eighteen."

He chuckled and said, "You better get yo' young ass to population so you can fight when you get frustrated. Shit. Sitting up here thinking about a damn girl gone' drive you crazy as hell. It's about time for trays to come. We got Salisbury cubes, mash potatoes, gravy, mixed veggies, and apple sauce. I'll talk to you later cu'."

I ate the potatoes and mixed veggies and saved the apple sauce for later. I put the tray in the door trap. I then heard the officer respond, "I'll come back and get you once I finish picking up the trays."

After hearing this encounter, I called down to OJ, "What's up Juice? What you 'bout to do?"

He said he was going to use the phone. "How in the hell did you pull that off?"

"You haven't used the phone?" he said, sounding shocked.

Honestly, I hadn't thought about using the phone with everything that was on my mind. "Nah, I haven't."

When the officer came to get Juice, he asked him to let me use the phone too. When we arrived in the phone room, I noticed that it was an old holding cell across from the visitation room. My thoughts went back to my emotional visit with mom, dad, and Angel. I waited, bubbling with excitement for my turn to use the phone. Who would I call?

There was only one place I knew where someone would be home—my parents' house. I was grateful OJ kept his call brief. When he hung up, I grabbed the phone and dialed my mother's number as fast as I could. The sound of my mother's voice made my heart dropped to my shoes. I was just as lost for words on the phone as I had been during our visit. I talked to mom for the entire twenty minutes and thanked her for coming to see me and bringing Angel.

She said she never imagined I could be put in such a serious situation, with my life literally in the hands of a system she knew nothing about. She and dad went to retain a lawyer earlier and she had no clue as to how they were going to pay him. The lawyer told them the last thing that I should be worrying about was a bond. The pain and frustration she felt vibrated through the phone into the core of my soul. Never in my life had I imagined that I could cause her so much pain by my wrongdoings. Just as I hung up, an officer rounded the corner to come take us back to our cells. He'd timed our allotted call time perfectly. I thanked OJ for putting me on game with the phone thing. Being in the hole, I didn't know that using the phone was even an option. I moped to my cell; blinded by despair I couldn't see the door's entrance—I just felt my way through. I only heard the loud *clank* from the lock as I slid past the barrier where I found comfort in my solitude and bunk.

Days passed and I had absolutely no desire to touch the phone, mentally traumatized by the anguish I'd dealt my parents. I decided I needed to escape from myself and one particular verse from *Ghetto Prisoners* by Nas played in my head constantly.

OJ knew the night before he got out that his stint in the hole was over, so we kicked it for a while, pulling nearly an all-nighter. An official all-nighter was staying up until the breakfast trays came.

"I know you got a lot on your mind cu but get your mind right and take yo ass to population. It ain't good to be locked up in this room too long!" he told me.

I promised him I'd get out as soon as I could figure it all out. After we called it a night, I tried to get comfortable in my bunk.

A scruffy voice woke me asking. "Are you eating breakfast this morning?"

I took my tray of food but had no appetite after waking up to the realization that this would be the routine of my life for a long time. The same damn runny oatmeal or hard grits, two pieces of soggy toast cut in half, stale cereal, one piece of quarter-sized sausage that I never attempted to taste, one milk, and some orange-colored juice.

After OJ returned to general population I went back to singing, rapping, writing, and playing "what if," a game I learned to play when I was four or five years old. I played it when I yearned for a better situation than the one I was in, like "what if my parents were rich." I could have better clothes. I played "what if" with my entire life in the confinement of that cell.

When I wasn't playing "what if," I read newspapers and put my thoughts on paper. There were others on the hall but no one I cared to converse with. I toyed with the Bible sometimes as mom had asked, but all I saw were words. I fought for some type of meaning and understanding, but received none, so I gave up. I figured some things aren't for everybody, so I took it that the Bible wasn't for me. I had entirely too much going on to decode its parables.

Around lunchtime, as the trays were coming, two officers brought me a new next-door neighbor. Apparently, he'd been fighting. His adrenaline looked to be pumping.

He was talking loud and fast to the officer that tussled him into his room. The officer matched his intensity, yet tried to calm him down at the same time. I guess they knew he was ignorant to the harm they could inflict upon him. Once he was inside, he began to yell and curse the officers out as if he was being victimized. As if that wasn't enough, he kicked the door until they came back with a third officer. They tried to calm him down by talking to him and eventually it worked. I think he finally realized the odds weren't in his favor. Once they left, he was quiet as a church mouse. I assumed it meant he fell asleep after a while. Must have worn himself out, exerting all that energy in such a short amount of time. That was my entertainment for the day.

I chilled out for a while and read my newspaper until they brought the dinner trays. I would hear the elevator ping, and the wheels on the tray cart shake and squeal when it was chow time. The squeal along with my next-door neighbor rapping aloud 2Pac's *Me and My Girlfriend* and banging on the wall woke me. We would later introduce ourselves, after we finished our meals, only after we both tried to get an extra tray. The food was usually horrible, but it was better to be full than hungry. I stuffed everything that I wanted to eat later into Styrofoam cups and wrapped the bread in paper napkins for later. I always sent empty trays back out.

My new next-door neighbor called himself "Philly" because he was from Philadelphia. He was two years younger than me, but he acted a lot younger than that. He told me he came to Wilson for the summer and somehow ended up with a murder charge. He said he wasn't really worried about it because he would beat it. As much as I didn't like to talk to him, we talked every meal and all night, except if we received any bad news or letters that day. He would tell me about his life in Philly and we would talk about things that we did on the streets of Wilson. I received nothing beneficial to me or for my well-being during those conversations, but they sure helped to pass the time.

One night after falling asleep mid-conversation, the rumbling hunger pains in my stomach shook me violently, forcing me awake. I heard Philly call my name, but I ignored him. I tried not to make too much noise because I didn't want to get caught up in another dialogue that shifted into a listening

12

session. Reaching for my food stash, I heard the elevator ping, and then a familiar voice. As the familiar voice and the officers walked past my cell, I saw it belonged to one of my older cousins' homeboys, Vinny.

"Mike, what's up?"

"Who dat?"

"Udy."

"Oh, shit. What's going on with you?"

"I came up here to get my thoughts together. What the hell you up here for?"

"Dem dudes wanted me out dat bitch 'cause I was gittin all da extra trays and I ain't smoke wit dey ass. I saw them eat and go scrap up while I was waiting on da officer to bring da tray back."

"What they strap up?" I asked.

"Oh, dey put on dey shoes, so dey cud jump me. I was scrapped up already, 'cause I knew dey was gone pump up der hearts soon and try me. When I was walking to da' table with my second tray and Knowledge fat ass swung on me and caught me in da shoulder. He lost his balance and Kell ended up in front of me. I caught Kell in da jaw and blood went pouring and he was terrified, so he ran to da bunk area to get a towel. Dre' bitch ass saw the blood and start calling da officer. Knowledge came and acted like he wanted to fight when the officers got in the block."

Two days later Vinny and I went to the concrete recreation center. There were no weights, basketball goals, or anything recreational to do other than get fresh air. It had no roof, so we were exposed to the outside elements. It was a reprieve from the stale smell of the building where there was a lack of circulating air.

We walked and talked for about four laps around the yard and he turned me on to the cigarette connection. Ten stamps would get you half a pouch of Top tobacco from the guys who came from the local prison who worked in the jail. Once Vinny got his tobacco, we hid and smoked a roll-up in the corner of the yard, as the jail was a non-smoking facility. I got lightheaded but needed that to take a load off. With every puff I released, I exhaled pain and frustration.

As we headed in the building and back to our cells, Vinny shoved a roll-up and some matches into my hand. I soon grew accustomed to sitting in my room, reading the newspaper, and smoking roll-ups after each meal.

Ten days flew by and Vinny was out of the hole. Before he got out, he told me to take my time to get my head right but that too much alone time wasn't good for anybody. I told him that I had been thinking about getting out soon anyway, so I would link up with him soon. Two people told me the same thing, so I guess it was time to really consider the idea.

I began to think to myself and realized that it was time for me to get out of here. I knew the rerun of what-ifs wasn't doing me any good—the reruns of what I lost and what and who I would miss. It was time to get out of my self-imposed solitude. The damnedest thing was that it wasn't as easy getting out of the hole as it was going in. Once I found an officer, I asked to speak the shift sergeant. He gave me the run around for a few days, but they finally moved me.

I had spent a month and a half in isolation. I finally made it to population, and I was ecstatic. The first face I saw was that of a crack addict I knew from the streets, smiling a rotten-toothed smile. As I entered the cell block, a stale smell assaulted my senses. It reminded me of my high school locker room. I stood in the bunk area and looked around until I found an open top bunk. As I checked out the block, I saw Vinnycovered up in his bunk. A couple of other guys were playing chess at a table and two more playing cards at another, while one guy was sitting on an ice cooler talking on the phone. The vision was by far clearer than it had been the first time I entered the cell after waking up on my first morning after being booked. The entire cell was bright, and I saw it through a different lens, now that my thoughts were unclouded.

Once I got settled in, talking, playing cards and board games, talking on the phone, and eating, nothing much changed. From time to time I wrote a letter and tried to express myself with my limited vocabulary. I had a G.E.D but no matter what they say, a G.E.D doesn't make you competitive in the world. It only says that for some reason you went back to school just to get closure.

I never knew just how little I knew until my cousin, Trauncey, recommended to my mom that I read *Black Boy* by Richard Wright. When I started reading, I purchased a dictionary from the canteen. It became my new best friend. Without it, I couldn't fully comprehend everything I was reading. Learning about Richard Wright and his life opened up a new reality. It showed me I knew absolutely nothing about nothing, and that humbled me.

When you walk around with other individuals that are oblivious to what's going on in the world, you don't have much to compare your intellect to. Once I completed *Black Boy*, Trauncey recommended *Manchild in the Promised Land* by Claude Brown, and then Malcolm X's autobiography. Reading helped me escape from my situation. With Richard, I traveled to Mississippi, Arkansas, Tennessee, and Chicago. I went to Harlem with Claude, and to Omaha, Milwaukee, Lansing, Roxbury, Flint, and Muslim countries with Malcolm. Their words began to shape and mold a new perspective for me.

Over the course of the next few months, the guys who were there when I first came in began to go to court or were sent prison, and some others went home. Newer guys would come in. Everyone was moving but me. I had become a permanent fixture. When dudes from my side of town came in, they always made their way to the cell I was in. Some other guys were repeat offenders who I grew cool with, and I would always make the processing officer bring them to my cell. We could catch up and they would bring me some cigarettes or weed. I always found it amazing how some guys could walk into jail with the same ease as they walked out of it.

More often than not, I was the youngest in the cell. For the most part, no one ever played on my youth. However, one day while playing cards with June-June, a guy maybe five years my senior, got frustrated and began to talk very belligerent.

"Lil nigga you can play cards, but can you play with these hands? It ain't no guns in here."

I was still trying to figure out where all this hate came from. I said, "I'm through," and dropped my cards on the table.

I walked into the bunk area, sat down, and started talking with an old head to get away from him. June-June stormed in, yelling at me. I did what I could to defuse his hostility, but realized it was time to get strapped up. June-June was slipping because he wasn't strapped up yet, too busy talking fight-talk. Once I was strapped up, I went straight to him and started throwing blows. I kept them coming non-stop. If I gave him an inch of breathing room to recover, it could turn the tables on me. An officer came by, saw me whaling on him and took me back to the hole.

When I got to the hole, my adrenaline slowed down, making me notice that my hand was throbbing and swollen. All I could do was cry from the pain. I banged on the door until the officer came and showed him my hand. He took me to see the nurse. She glanced at it, barely touched it, said it wasn't broken and dismissed me. On the way back to the hole, the officer gave me a bag of ice and a couple packs of Tylenol. I took them, grateful for the gesture, and balled up in a fetal position on my bunk. Looking at the ceiling in agony, I played back every lousy decision I'd made in life that led me to where I was. The playback, the ice or the Tylenol did not calm the pulsating pain that inflated my hand with every beat of my heart. I closed my eyes and relived my first jail scuffle instead and it brought me relief. Knowing that I kicked June-June's ass gave me a small moment of bliss, enough that I smiled and was able to fall asleep.

Since I had been in the block for so long when I was released from the hole, D-102 was my destination. When I walked in, I was given a warm welcome back from a group of the guys who were there when I had left. However, Vinnywas in the greeting circle and he wasn't there before I went to the hole. We locked eyes and he tilted his head while smirking.

Vinnysaid, "Damn child support."

He prepared a stash just in case the judge didn't rule in his favor that day. He brought in cigarettes, so we sat up all night, smoking, talking, and playing cards. We talked about what was going on in the streets and what's been going on in the county. Once breakfast was served, I gulped down my food and went to sleep. Just like that our welcome back party was over and so I retired for the day.

I didn't tell Vinnyabout the horrific news that I've been holding in since I received it earlier in the week. My girlfriend Angel had a miscarriage. I didn't know how to deal with it so it was just something else for me to compartmentalize, and act as if it didn't exist.

After Vinnywas back in the block for a couple of weeks, one of his partners came to the block. Nuke was 6' 3", athletic built, a 5 percenter that didn't eat meat. Since I'd been introduced to the 5 percenter teachings, Nuke and I used that common ground to build an alliance. As always, I was the youngest of the bunch, so they treated me like their little brother. We hustled stamps, cigarettes, and canteen items together. We ended up fighting together too.

The fight ended up getting us all assault charges. It started when a guy named Mont transferred in from Rocky Mount to face the remainder of his charges in Wilson. He was from Wilson and honestly, I always thought of him as crazy as hell because when I was in high school, he snuck in and beat the

19

hell out of a student. Not to mention that there was a rumor that he had shot himself in the head with a .22 caliber gun. When Mont came to the cell, he had on some boots that reeked of stagnant sewer water.

"Yo, G, can you move your boots from the head of my bunk?" Nuke asked.

"Man, my boots ain't bothering nobody. Why don't you want to move nobody shit but mine?"

"Your joints must be damp or something G, 'cause they got an odor. I ain't trying to play you. They in my face when I lay down."

"Well if you want them out of your face, you move em'."

"Bet, I'm going to put them in the dayroom," Nuke said and put them in a plastic bag, tied it up, and put them in the dayroom.

Mont let it go until we start playing cards. He started getting mouthy toward Nuke and they were even on the same spades team. Mont threw the cards and told Nuke to strap up and he did. Vinnyand I did as well. Once Mont saw what was happening, he swung first to no avail. Vinnymade the first connection and Nuke and I followed his suit. We threw punches and kicked in a lopsided brawl even after seeing a puddle of blood on the floor. I was so lost in making Mont feel my frustration with each blow that I didn't hear the door open.

I felt someone grab me and lift me from my zone. The officers handcuffed me, Mike, and Nuke, and took us to a holding cell in booking. We stayed in there for hours, long enough to strategize a plan. We knew the officers would make Mont press charges, so Nuke and Vinnysaid they would take the charges and tell them that I was breaking it up since I was facing serious charges already. The officers would hear none of it, so we all got new misdemeanor assault charges. Once we were given our papers from the magistrate, we were taken back to our block, which was a shocker since we were looking to go to the hole.

When we got back, all the other guys were gone. It was just the three of us to ourselves. All we did was read and play solitaire, chess, and sleep. They didn't move anyone in the block for two weeks. We couldn't go to the yard, couldn't get any cigarettes, so we were cranky and spoke very little to each other after a week. They slowly began to bring others in, which cut the tension in the air. Within the next month, Nuke and Vinnywere bonded out, but they left with the new charge to face. They failed to go to court for our fight charge and came back shortly after posting bail. The system always seemed to be a revolving door for so many. After they did their time for the fight, they went home free. My charges were dismissed because of the severity of my initial charges.

As my court date grew near, I began to obsess over what would happen. I knew all the daily games were to come to a halt and gain focus on my life. My birthday had passed. I was nineteen, but felt more like twenty-nine. I'd begun to grow facial hair. Angel, ShiRon, Isha, and Denise had all gotten on with their lives and I couldn't blame them. There was no single thing or event, but rather an array of poor decisions that had lead me to this point. The desire to fit in and yet do my own thing—the ambiguity of my life—was the driving force behind me in the county jail with my life in the hands of a system that I didn't trust and certainly didn't understand.

May 15th in the year 2000, I woke up early with every type of knot and butterfly in my stomach. It was the day I would learn my fate. The officer came in at 7 and brought me the clothes that my family had sent for me to wear to court. He told me I had to be in court by 7:30 because court started at 8. Once I got dressed, it seemed as if it took all day for him to come back for me. The guys in the block were somber and gave me words of encouragement. When the door finally popped open, I thought my heart would pop as well. My legs felt as if I had two 45-pound weights tied to each of them, and I still had to put on shackles and handcuffs. When we finally reached the holding cell (bullpen), other guys were already packed in, waiting to learn their destiny as well.

Once the judge entered and court began, the officers started calling us in according to the docket. My case wasn't called until 9:30. All I could do was sit and wait, watching other guys come and go. When I entered the courtroom, I looked around and made eye contact with everyone: my mom, dad, sister and other family members. I saw a couple of my homies who had come to show their support too. I saw the pain again on my mother's face, as she tried to crack a smile for me. I sat down and knew my question was about to be answered in a few minutes.

"The State of North Carolina versus Ronald M. Bullock!" The words rattled my soul.

How in the hell was I going to win this shit! I stood up and walked timidly toward my lawyers. I had two of Wilson's best, Toby Fitch and Robert Farris. They whispered to each other and then began to plead my case. The judge, Frank Brown, listened as if he already had his mind made up to what my numbers were. The next time I heard him speak, his voice sounded like Charlie Brown's teacher's. After the mumbling was over, I was escorted out of the courtroom. I didn't know what had just happened until Mr. Farris ran me down and asked if I understood. I didn't and so I shook my head, feeling numb.

"You were sentenced to 154 to 204 months, which would leave you with a little more than eleven years to do," he said.

23

"Ok. When will I leave?" is all I could think to ask. I knew I'd be transferred to a state prison.

"You should leave in the next day or two. If you need anything, just have your family contact me." As quick as he appeared, he vanished.

I was led back to the cell and jumped on the phone to call Angel to tell her what had happened. The whole county heard that I had gone to court, so when I got back a couple of guys hollered through the vents to hear the outcome. I talked for a while, and then went to lie down. I couldn't keep my eyes open all of a sudden. The block was still somber when I woke up, but a guy in the cell had some weed and he smoked a joint with me. We played cards and talked shit all night. I tried all I could but there was no escaping the fact that I had an amount of time on my plate that I wasn't ready to eat yet. The weed and the card games were only temporary. The reality was what it was and there was no escaping it.

When I woke up the next morning for breakfast, I couldn't get the phone to work. I wanted to call my mother before she left to go to work that morning. For some reason, I didn't even notice that this was a sign that I was leaving that day. I'd seen the phones get turned off before when they were shipping someone out. My mind wasn't clear because I had just added up my sentence. I had almost twelve years left! After we finished eating, I tried to call home again, but the phones were still off.

Out of the blue, I heard, "Ronald Bullock, bag and baggage!"

Since the day of my arrival a year ago to the date, I'd been waiting to hear that sentence. Now that I'd heard it, I dreaded it. I knew the move would forever change my whole life. When I'd hoped to hear it, I had thought I would be going home, but that was because I still hadn't accepted the consequences of my actions.

Somewhere in the midst of that dread, I decided, before it comes to an end, it first has to start. So I thought, "Fuck it. Let's get it started."

I made a vow that I would leave a boy, but would return to Wilson County as a man. My first sentence had come to an end. It was time to start a new chapter.

Chapter 2

DROPPED OFF AND LOST

I was on the way to prison, "the big house," Polk Youth Institution. I followed the officer to the booking room where I was handed my personal belongings that I had on me the night of my arrest—my wallet and a pack of Newport 100s. I was then taken to a connecting room where two other guys were being handcuffed and shackled. It was Boo and Donny, two guys that I had known from my middle school days. Once we were all chained and restrained, we had an armed escort to our waiting van.

Lieutenant Barnes oversaw all transportation for the county and he just so happened to be our driver. He was known for his candid demeanor and his no-nonsense attitude. Officer Brown, the maternalistic gentle giant, accompanied him for the ride. No matter how bad you felt when you saw Ms. Brown, her aura always forced you to smile.

Once we were all packed in, our journey to prison began. The three of us indulged in small talk in between falling asleep every so often. I looked out of the window in awe of the freedom of the trees and nature. I was just trying to wrap my mind around the unknown and prepare myself for what I was about to face for the next twelve years.

After riding for what seemed like days from Wilson to Butner, I was ready for the next part of my journey to begin. As we finally approached our barbed wire–enclosed fortress, I wasn't sure what to expect other than a good fight. I knew there'd be the inevitable physical brawls, but the mental battle would be my first challenge.

As we exited the white county transfer van, three prison guards, two black and one white, all had on Carolina blue button-up shirts and dark blue pants. They conversed with the county officers as if sharing information.

Then out of nowhere the shorter plump black officer came from his gut with, "Pull your damn pants up boy!"

I wasn't sure who his words were directed at, but all three of us obeyed his command.

"Oh, we got someone here that loves when you wear your pants down on your ass," the white officer said.

The third officer who was slim and taller than the other at about 6' 3" smirked and added his two cents. "It's all good sergeant. They're about to take all that shit off anyway!"

As the county officers exchanged our files and paperwork with the prison officers, Officer Brown whispered, "I'll tell your mom that you're here."

It gave me a sense of relief to know that mom would know exactly where I was in the world because I didn't know when I'd get to use a phone. When the county officers left, I felt the vibration of the gray door as it closed. Suddenly, the room grew warm and moist.

"Boy, this is the beginning of the next 12 years of my life," I muttered to myself.

"Shut up! I didn't tell you to talk," the slim officer said.

"Don't get scared now," the white one added, chuckling.

I felt embarrassed and I knew my face showed it. Maybe it showed everything that I wanted to conceal.

"Slim" started toward a green door and said, "Ok, little girls, I need you to follow me. I'll give you three boxes. Write your home address or wherever the hell you want to send this shit. Or you can donate it. I don't give a damn where it goes!"

The three of us followed him like sheep being led to slaughter. I was the first one to enter the room Slim directed us to. Showerheads lined the drab gray wall. Behind us, on a concrete slabbed bench, there were blue half bars of "state

28

soap", thin generic white wash rags, towels, grayish-brown pants, dingy white shirts, boxers, socks and white shoes. People called those white shoes "BBCs," "Bo-Bos", or simply "state shoes."

"Take your street clothes off. You're now inmates and belong to the North Carolina department of corrections. Put your shit in these boxes, seal the box, wash your ass, and put on your state clothes that you were issued," Slim said and walked away, as if he had told his child to clean their room.

After my shower, I got dressed and waited for the next demeaning order to be barked at us. As I stood waiting, I tried to slow down my mind. It had been racing all day. In-processing seemed to take hours. I wanted out of that musty room and to smoke a cigarette.

"Big Rob," the white officer yelled.

A dark-skinned officer as wide as a door marched over. The name below his badge read, *Robinson*. Two inmates flanked him on each side—one black, the other white. Big Rob turned to the black guy, short and athletic with shoulder-length dreads. "Hey Lucky, fix me three mattress covers so we can get these clowns outta here!"

The white inmate had a blonde buzz cut and was Ramen noodle-thin. He pulled a trash bag out of his back pocket and lined the can. Both inmates were dressed in fresh sets of brown pants, white tees, and white Chuck Taylor converses. Lucky gave us our mattress covers, which held three changes of clothing, a towel, washcloth, and a bedroll (sheets, pillow, pillowcase, and a blue blanket), and a state hygiene kit. The hygiene kits contained a clear Bob Barker deodorant, a small tube of Bob Barker toothpaste, a small toothbrush, and Bob Barker shampoo. After that we were marched across the compound to make our grand entrance.

We saw other inmates going on with their daily activities. Some were dressed in all white, pushing huge metal carts. Some were cutting grass with old-school hand-powered lawnmowers. Others were walking around with bags in their hands, picking up trash. I noticed the difference in their apparel compared to mine, Boo, and Danny's. Our clothes were shabbier.

When we finally got to our dorms, they put Boo and me in the same block and Donny in the adjoining block. The smell of the air was funky, dry, and damp, reminiscent of when I first got out of the hole in the county.

"Hey, new jacks. This is ya'll's bunk number," the dorm officer called, standing in the doorway. He reached in, handing us sticky notes with our number written on them.

I roamed around the block aimlessly with my sticky note, refusing to ask anyone for help. Comparing my number to those written on empty bunks, I kept walking after each mismatch.

A brawny guy viciously brushing his hair approached and asked, "Whut bunk ya lookin fo' my man?" He extended his hand and added, "Bookworm from the Port City."

"Udy, bunk 14," I replied and shook his hand.

"Where ya from my man?"

"Wilson."

"Wide-A-Wake, huh? So, where ya dreads at? Or you cut em' fa court?"

"Nah, I never had dreads."

"Did they give ya any B-news?"

"What the hell is a B-new? Where you say you from again?" I didn't understand what I assumed was prison lingo.

"I'm from the Port City, Wilmington, and a B-new is a brand-new shirt."

"Man, I really don't know what's in that bag."

"Ya smoke? Ya want a cig? It's on me."

I contemplated long and hard because I recalled all of the horror stories that I'd heard about accepting things from people in prison. I wasn't going to let anyone chump me. That could lead to a rough twelve years.

My dad's voice rang loud and clear. "Stand up for yourself. Fight when you got to. I only had two daughters and I expect it to stay like that."

The dude was wearing flip-flops with no socks. That alone told me I could handle myself if something was wrong with what he was offering, so I ignored the warnings.

"Hell, yeah. Let me get one."

"Ya got to smoke in the smoking section. If ya got a B-new, I'll shoot ya two mo."

I picked my mattress cover off the floor and threw it on my bunk. Bookworm met me with a cigarette in the smoking section. I sat in one of the four plastic armchairs and lit my cigarette. The first inhale made me lightheaded but I still found a way to smoke half of it before I called Boo over to offer him the rest. I returned to my bunk, began to unpack, and called Bookworm over to see if I had any new shirts. I found one and so we made an exchange for the smokes he promised.

While on the yard some guys lifted weights, others played basketball, volleyball, or horseshoes. Others walked around in cliques and groups. I noticed there was a line for the canteen. Watching the activity of the line, I saw that some people would get their things and then go give them to others. I wondered what was going on, so I continued to watch. The buyers all acted timid, and the takers (the people they gave the stuff to) all seemed intimidating. It wasn't difficult to put two and two together. It was a classic example of the strong ruling the weak.

I was far from weak and even farther from being susceptible to extortion. Neither my parents nor the streets of Wilson had raised a willing victim.

Boo, Donny, and I walked around the yard and tried to wrap our minds around being in prison. We were in orientation, so we had a lot of appointments ahead of us in the following week. We smoked cigarettes, talked about the streets, playing sports in school, and the women who we were writing to. We tried to prepare ourselves for all that was ahead of us. My road would be a lot longer than theirs, but at that point, we were all we had.

The yard closed and the guards herded us back into our blocks to prepare to be called to the chow hall. The two guards working the dorm called each of the four blocks, one by one, and we lined up accordingly. Each block held approximately fifty inmates. There were two sides to each dorm. That's four hundred young men between the ages of eighteen and twenty-one, young, misguided, mad at the world, raging bulls full of testosterone. To top that off there were Bloods, Crips, Folks, Sur-13, MS-13, Latin Kings, 5 percenters, Muslims, Christians, people all from different cities. The list goes on. Everyone had to find something to identify with. It was in these chow hall lines where a lot of the fights and extortion took place. Somehow only five officers prepared all of us to get in line and walk us to chow. As we entered the chow hall, an officer split the line down the middle, making half of us go through one door and the other half through another.

The place was huge. There were two sides, fifty tables on each side. Each table had four seats. There was a control booth where someone sat who opened the doors and a sergeant stood in the middle aisle, barking orders. He had a system that didn't allow any talking. He said if you were talking, you couldn't possibly be hungry and then he'd kick you out. When it was my turn, the inmate working the serving line asked what I wanted to eat. I stared at him like he was speaking another language. I had options? Back at the county jail, the tray you were given was your only option.

"Yo! What the hell do you wanna eat?" the guy asked again. "It don't matter." I was so used to not having a choice, it didn't.

He threw some chicken stew on my tray, and I followed the guy in front of me, trying to act as natural as possible. I got to my seat and ate the side dishes and dessert. I was still practicing vegetarianism since meeting Nuke. I didn't want to talk and risk getting caught on my first day. Once I finished, I took my tray up to the garbage window past the yelling sergeant and followed the other guys back to the dorm. When we got back, an officer told us the showers were open.

The showers were set up with four showerheads in a stall two on two facing walls. In my entire life, I had never taken a shower with a male person other than during the in-processing a few hours prior. I was sure I would never get used to it. I opted out, still feeling clean from the one I'd taken earlier. I went to the smoking area instead, caught a short off someone, and then went back to my bunk to gather my thoughts. Laying on my bunk, I realized I'd finished my first day in prison. Only 4,379 more to go, no weekends off.

Over the next few days, we were called to medical to get physicals, health diagnostics, and psychiatric evaluations. The next week we met our case managers. Boo and Donny were told they would be shipped out to minimum custody camps soon, since they both had less than a year on their sentences. I, on the other hand, was assigned to the D.A.R.T (drug abuse rehabilitation treatment) block and told I would stay at Polk until I turned twenty-one. Two and a half years. I needed to put together a plan for how that time would go.

Within the next week, I was relocated to the D.A.R.T block. It was set up just like the last block. Fifteen bunks downstairs and about sixteen bunks upstairs with a bathroom right in front of the bunk area. There was a small dayroom with tables for playing games, a TV, and a smoking area.

I didn't know anyone and this time no one approached me with any propositions like Bookworm had. I put my things in my locker and made up my bunk. I had money on my canteen-card, so I was able to buy cigarettes and a Walkman.

After stowing my things, I locked my locker and snatched my Walkman. Grabbing a chair from the stack, I found a spot in the dayroom and did some "people watching."

I didn't belong in a drug treatment program. I'd never used anything other than weed and drank alcohol only occasionally. Yet, I had to take classes on the dangers of drugs and talk about how they had affected my life. The next day I was called to the counselor's office. When I arrived, I saw a large dark-skinned lady with a colorful blouse on.

"You gotta be Bullock, sit down."

"Yes, ma'am."

"Bullock, I gonna shoot straight from the hip with you. I've seen your kind before. You are full of shit."

"Where did that come from," I asked.

"See! You gone try to bullshit your way through my program and the system. I promise you, it's not going to work on me. Ms. Williamson is known as the breaker and I'm going to break you from your bullshit."

When she spoke in third person, I was sold. Ms. Williamson was nuts. She continued her rant about my addictive habits ruling me. I guess she was right because I had wanted some weed right then and there.

She ended the rant with, "Oh, you gone feel me, even if you don't hear me." Just like that, I was dismissed.

On my way back to the block I walked past the canteen line and stopped to get some chips and a drink. Just as I completed my purchase, a voice came from over my shoulder.

"What the hell are you doing, inmate! Who told you to go to ma' canteen?" A brown-skinned, medium-built officer yells.

"Nobody," I said. "I just left Ms. Williamson's office, so I stopped to grab me something since it was open."

He said, "Come to ma office."

"I told you that you were going to bullshit your way through the system," Ms. Williamson said as she waddled down the hall dressed like a bed of flowers.

"Close ma door son."

"What's ya name an' where ya from new jack," he asked in a rapid pace.

"Ron Bullock, from Wilson."

"Ok Ron, I'm Sergeant Daniels. I ain't seen ya before and ya jus jumpin in ma damn canteen line, so ya ass got ta' be a new jack. Look here, ya can take this for what its worf. I'm gone give ya a little survival one-oh-one before ya lil ass gets too comfortable an' thank ya know every damn thang."

"Ok"

"Stay ya ass out dem damn gangs. Get all tha' free education ya can. It'll keep ya out of trouble. An when ya get out, what ya learned gone keep ya ass out. Its jus that simple."

37

"Thanks," was all I could think to say.

"I'm gone see ya round. I hate ta see all ma young brothas in here wastin' time not learnin shit. I'll let ya go on this, ya the only one that can decide how ya do ya time." He shook my hand and I went back to my block.

My first time having a civilized exchange with an officer since my introduction to Polk. I wasn't sure of his intentions. I was sure that he had offered some wisdom to take along my journey.

During my first couple of days in the classroom setting, we looked at the movie "Temptations" which was great because I wasn't mentally prepared for any type of classroom work. The only catch was we had to write a paper on the movie once we were finished. I had no clue where to begin. I was five years removed from my ninth-grade education.

I consulted with the peer counselors to get some advice on writing and the class as a whole. I began to mingle and talk with others in the class, settling into the environment. I started to like Ms. Williamson. She was funnier than I had gathered from our first meeting.

Our desks were arranged in a circle and at the beginning of each session, we recited the serenity prayer before proceeding with whatever the daily topic was. I was amazed by the number of young guys addicted to hard drugs like crack, meth, heroin, prescription drugs, and the list go on. How these drugs actually consumed them was amazing. It intrigued me, so I began to ask questions about their lives and how they got to that point.

My parents had just got the long-distance feature back on their phone plan so I could call home. My mother told me that she and my father would be coming to see me on Sunday. I was so excited I couldn't talk anymore. For the next two days, I walked on thin ice. I didn't want any mishaps to cause me to not be able to get that visit.

Saturday, I watch TV, played chess, and took a shower. I found the best-looking pair of brown pants and the cleanest shirt I could, and went to bed early. I locked my locker and listened to the quiet storm slow jams until I found sleep. When I woke up my radio was gone. I looked for it under my pillow since I'd fallen asleep on it, but it wasn't there nor were the keys to my locker. I tore my bed up to find them, but no radio and no keys.

I jumped off the top bunk and saw that my lock was gone too. I was at a loss for words because everything I had tried to dodge was now happening. There was an unspoken code to not go to the guards with something like this, but I knew if I let it go, I would be a marked man. My sentence would be tough for the remainder of my stay.

I went to breakfast and pulled a couple of guys to the side, trying to get a little information. I talked to the dorm janitor and everyone had the same story. They knew nothing. I went in and ate a little, but my appetite was shot. My mind was racing, trying to figure out when and how I was going to solve my problem. I hadn't really forged a relationship with anyone to gather any real information. On my way back to the dorm, a little white guy found his way to me and introduced himself.

"What's up mi boi, I heard ya sayin ya locka got hit last night."

"Yeah, they was nice as fuck too. I had my headphones in my ear, and my keys was under my pillow." I stuck out my hand to shake his. "Udy," I said.

"Ice."

"So you know who got my shit?"

"Nah mi boi. I got connections. Imma Folk my people run shit." He said while showing me some type of hand gestures.

"Well, I just need to know who got my shit," I said, while thinking I wish they would just return it without any problems.

"If I can't point ya in da right direction, I know somebody that will sell ya ah lock and a radio."

"Bet, I got a visit later. I just want my shit on my bunk when I get back."

"I got ya mi boi. Imma see what I can find out for you."

We were finished talking by the time we reached my bunk. I jumped on it and stared at the ceiling, waiting for my name to be called for visitation.

Visitation started at 9 o'clock and my name was one of the first to be called. I had the urge to address the entire block before I left. I wanted to yell, "When I get back I want my things on my bunk!" Then I would walk out to go see my family, but I didn't. I walked out with my wheels turning and heart racing.

When I reached the visitation hall, an officer checked me in. He checked each inmate's items that they were taking into visitation so nothing extra would be taken out by anyone. I walked into the crowd of faces and began to search for the ones that I loved so dearly.

"Udy, over here." I followed the voice and spotted my mom waving her short arm trying to get my attention. We locked eyes, walked toward each other, and hugged as if our next breath depended on our connection. She led me back to our table where Nic-Nic my sister, Dee, and Jay my nephews were waiting.

"I kinda figured you wanted a Snicker and a Sprite," Nic-Nic said.

"Thanks. You know those are my favorites."

"How's everything going, son? You lookin good."

"Thanks, beautiful. It's in my DNA. I'm good though."

"Fo' some odd reason every time you say you *good*, yo lil mind be jus a racin'. Ya momma know ya, so what's on ya mind?"

"You know me, huh?"

"Yep, what's goin' on?"

"My radio and lock got stolen last night, but don't worry about nothing. I met this guy this morning that said that he would help me find it."

"Lord, watch ova my baby! Do what you feel is necessary, Lord. Jus be careful."

"I told you that the dude was going to help me. I'm good. Where is daddy and how is he doing?"

41

"He is at home waiting on the Cowboy's game. He told us to tell you what's up and he love ya."

I knew that my news would damper the vibe of my visit, so I made small talk with Dee and Jay about school, and with Nic-Nic about her job at the bank. It was too late though. I had ruined the visit and I knew there was nothing I could do to ease the tension. Somewhere during our awkward silence, the officer interrupted with his "visitation is over" announcement. I hugged everyone, saving my mom for last.

"I love you and I'll write you and let you know how it all play out," I said.

"Ok, baby jus be careful. I love you more than you will ever know."

They made their exit and left me seated to play the what-if game.

After all of the visitors left, we were left in the visitation area to wait to be searched before we returned to our dorms. That was the longest trek to the dorm ever. Entering the dorm, I prayed that my radio and lock would be on my bunk and everything would be figured out for me. But honestly, why would someone take their time to steal it if they were just going to return it? I was a nobody. No one knew me and I hadn't done anything for anyone to know me. Slowly, approaching the dorm, the officer in the control booth opened the door for me to enter and next to enter the block. If it is possible for a million thoughts to occupy your mind all at once, I think I experienced it at that very moment. I tried to observe everyone's actions while I

42

was walking toward my bunk. No one showed their hand, so I continued to my bunk only to find it empty.

I walked into the bathroom and Ice was washing his hands. "What's good my boi. I got a trail on yo shit."

Just as soon as he got shit out of his mouth, my fist followed. The first punch he fell against the wall and I followed up until he fell. I kicked him until a group of officers rushed through the door and grabbed me. While I was beating him, he says that the radio was in his locker. Someone heard him and grabbed it for me and put it on my bed.

I was handcuffed and taken to the sergeant's office and asked what it was all about. I told them, and they took me back to the block to roll my bedroll up and go to segregation. I was happy that I went with my gut. It was a good thing that I had actually sat back and watched the same scenario play out just a week prior to me moving to D.A.R.T. The guy that did the stealing was also the negotiator. It worked in my favor to be observant.

My time in segregation was a breeze. I couldn't have my radio to listen to, but the library cart came around and I checked out a John Grisham book. I initially checked it out to pass time but somehow it was very entertaining, so it only lasted a day and a half. I checked out two more books the following day, enjoying the relaxation and solitude. I thought of my mother's face when I told her about the situation, so I decided to write her and thank her for all that she has done and the sacrifices that she made for me, a real heartfelt letter. I tried to think about what the next eleven years held for me, but I had no clue. I couldn't wrap my mind around being in prison that long. It was the year 2000 and I was waiting for 2012.

After I had completed my time in segregation, I was sent to the dorm that I had started in, but was put in a different block. When I got there, I knew absolutely no one at all, so I felt a little uncomfortable knowing that I was in a strange land and had no lock on my locker.

"What's up homie? What dorm did you come from?" A tall, slinky guy asked, looking under his hair as he undid his braids.

"I just came from the hole."

"I heard you from Wide-A-Wake. My people told me how things went down in the other block."

I assumed that his question was an icebreaker because he knew who I was before I set foot in the dorm. He said his name was TB, and that he was one of the leaders of the Bloods and called shots on the yard.

"Do you know my lil man Snot? We were in training school together."

"Yeah, that's my dude. He is still in the county, hopefully, he won't make it to state!"

Part of this was a lie because Snot and I weren't really seeing eye to eye at that moment, but I did want him to beat his charge and bypass prison. We kicked it about Snot and what was going on in the dorms. We then went our separate ways and I went back through the making up my bunk routine all over again.

I was a little more at ease after kicking it with TB, yet I had more questions about how he knew so much about me and where I was from. I decided I would bring it up some other time. About a week later, a sergeant and two officers came into our block and escorted TB out. I wasn't sure what was going on because hours later a couple of officers came back and packed his belongings and left. I later found out that they said that he put a hit on someone in the single cells. It showed me how fast things could change.

I quickly grew tired of the block because all we did was watch TV, smoke cigarettes, play dominos, chess, and sleep. Every day there was a fight, a check-off (someone realizing they are a sheep amongst wolves and telling the sergeant that they have to be moved), or a locker break-in (which is the reason someone would check-off). One day while lying on the bunk in the sweltering heat, I heard the door open and a small voice call out my name along with a list of others. I looked over the tier to see what was going on and what I was being called for. It was Ms. Baily, the counselor in charge of job placement, holding a piece of paper. She followed up the name-calling with instructions.

"Put on your shoes, grab your I.D. card, and come with me." Once we got outside, she told us that we were going to the clothes house to get some boots, so we could go to work. "You all going to work in the kitchen. Some first shift, the others second. I know a lot of you are not trying to work in the kitchen but that's tough luck! You can refuse and go to segregation and I'll assign you right back to the kitchen once you get out of segregation."

There was a total of four of us and I was the only one assigned to first shift. We arrived at the clothes house to get our boots. It was my first time in there and with all of the wet and dirty clothes came along a moist and musty stench. The clothes house worker fished me out a size eleven out of the mound of black boots that had been thrown into a pile without the slightest bit of order. He sprayed the boots off with a spray bottle of all-purpose cleaner and then handed them to me. I took them hesitantly and looked around at the other guys and how they responded to getting some dirty ass boots sprayed with some all-purpose cleaner. They received their boots with no problem too. Shit, some guys didn't have anything other than the state-issued B.B.C.'s or their flip-flops. It was good that they finally got some foot support.

Once we got our boots, we were issued four white pants and shirt jackets. Of course, the supposed-to-be-white clothes were dingy and reeked with a faint smell of old food. It turned my stomach to hold the clothes so close to me. This had to be one of the worst experiences of receiving clothes since I got here. I needed to build a relationship with someone in the clothes house soon. Once we got our clothes, Ms. Bailey escorted us back to our dorms and told us that we would be moving to the single cells once the second shift officers came in. I was kind of excited about moving to the single cells; however, I wasn't thrilled at all about having to work in the kitchen seven days a week.

"The single cells," I whispered under my breath, captivated by the three tiers with twelve rooms on each floor. I quickly understood why everyone wanted to get a job. It was so they could get there. The dayroom was huge, but there weren't a lot of people out. Many were in their rooms resting. I found my cell, set my room up, and then got someone to help me put my mattress in the mattress cover. Once settled, I went out and chilled in the dayroom to get a feel of the people in my new block. The TV had on some program, but I wasn't watching or listening. I ran the scan on my radio channels to see which stations came in clear on this side of the prison compound.

I heard the outside sliding door open and a group of guys came in. Some came in my block, others went to the other three blocks. I watched the door to see who I knew from other dorms. The only person I recognized was the tall, slim, white guy named J. J from Port City. We locked eyes and made sure that we had a positive identity and dapped each other. He called me Wilson, which caused some of the other guys to barrage me with questions about if I knew certain people from there. One short guy with dreads stepped close and asked me if I knew of a cat named Dirty Lue. I wasn't sure I knew him by that name, so I asked him to describe him or give me his "government name." He said his real name then.

"Hell yeah. That's my dude," I said.

"Well, as long as we are together, if you need anything, just let me know. Dirty Lue showed me mad love at the High Rise and looked out for me when no one else would, not even my homeboys."

We shook hands with an embracing hug. He introduced himself as "lil-Tee." We kicked it until the yard opened and then we ran out to try to get in front of the canteen line. He gave me a few pointers when we were in line, like going to bed early because 4 o'clock comes fast. Make sure that my nails were clean and short. Ms. Downing, one of the head officers in the kitchen, would check them each morning. We talked about everyday prison life and the things we wanted to pursue. During our walk, he was asked the same question a couple of times by different people: "Is he family?" "Is he six?"

He gave the same answer each time. "Nah, Gee. Dis Dirty Lue homeboy."

I didn't ask any questions but, I knew I couldn't get too tight with him. The last thing I wanted was to get caught up in gang business.

After being awakened at 3:30 am and marched to the chow hall by what seemed like half the officers on the compound. We were lined up on the wall where Ms. Downing barked orders at us. First, she made us count ourselves then we held out our hands so she and another officer could check our fingernails. She reached me, said my nails needed to be cut, and sent me to the office with two others. We were given a fingernail clipper, but I bit mine. I didn't know any of the guys who were using it nor did I know any of the previous guys from years prior who has used the same clipper.

When I went back out into the dining area, the guys were standing in line waiting to get their trays. When lil Tee saw me, he walked to the back of the line with me to tell me, "I told you."

After we ate, I was told I would be working in the tray room for a while. My job was to take the tray after each person was finished, dump the remaining contents, and put them in a rack to be washed. This required a lot of patience because the trays came in fast and periodically a smartass would throw his tray in and break my concentration. I worked the tray room for two days, and then I was moved to pots and pans since I couldn't get coordinated enough to get the routine down. Pots and pans were a slower pace, so I was cool with the spot. It just so happened that J. J was over there already so I knew it would be a laid-back gig. The job required me to wash the pots and pans or rinse, dry, and stack them.

While I was being trained on the process, I heard someone call out my name in an unsure tone. I located the voice and saw that it was Razor, my homeboy, smiling as he looked through the tray room window. We talked for a while until the sergeant patrolling the dining area kicked him out and told Ms. Downing on me. When she came to get me, I was back in my area, but, boy, did she let me have it. She got loud and used every curse word known to man. I was embarrassed at first, but let it go and got on with my work.

After working together for two weeks, J. J and I came up with a system. We alternated our daily duties. One day I'd wash and he dried, the next day vice versa. We decided this would make it feel like one workday and one chill day. Hamburger day was one of our most dreaded though. We quickly learned that while they were one of the easiest things to cook, they were the most difficult thing to clean off of the pans. The pans had to be soaked for a while and then scrubbed viciously. The time and effort it took to clean the sheet pans always caused J. J. and me to have to work late

J. J was blessed with not only hamburgers on one of his wash days one week, but the ultimate worst, cheeseburgers, on his next turn! We learned to get the pans off the line early so we could start soaking them as soon as possible. It was all good until J.J started washing and the cheese became a problem.

"Yo, Udy we gotta switch for the day."

I acted like I didn't hear him. I continued to sanitize and dry the dishes, but thought to myself, "He bugging."

"Yo, Udy, I'm not doing this shit today. So, you may as well get ready to wash for the rest of the day," he added, sounding annoyed.

I ignored him again, not liking his tone. I didn't have anything to lose at the time, nothing to look forward to other than keeping my mother worry-free. (I had no medium custody review, no job that I wanted, wasn't going home anytime soon...)

I said, "If you want me to wash them dishes you got me fucked up." I said it from my gut and it felt good. I had on those thick rubber gloves to keep my hands from getting scalded while dipping the dishes in the 100-degree sanitizing sink. As I waited for a response, I plotted a way to take them off without him noticing; I left to get some water and when I came back, I left them off for a while. I waited on him to start his rant again, but he must have come across some easy pans because he started a normal conversation. Just as I calmed down, he started ranting again. I felt the vibe between us shift so I went to the restroom to have a reason to remove my gloves again.

"You keep leaving, I'm going to be drying when you come back, pussy ass nigga," I heard him say as I walked away.

As I walked down the hall to the restroom, I tried to get my anger under control. I wanted to think clearly when I went back onto the floor. When I left the bathroom, I stopped by the cooking area to holla at lil Tee. We joked a little bit before Ms. Downy came.

J. J saw me approaching and said, "Are you ready, pussy?"

I was glad he started before I put my gloves on. I invaded his comfort zone and hit him with every inch of anger, frustration, hate, confusion, and muscle I had in my soul. On contact, he was asleep. I dived on him and blacked out. Just as soon as I blacked out I was quickly snapped back. I was grabbed by the neck and slammed by a big white officer who put his knee in my back, pulled my little dreads so he could unload his mace can. I'm sure had he had a gun, he would have made a "mistake." I was rushed to segregation to be washed off and then thrown in a cell with nothing but the wet clothes that I had on.

I was then sent to modified segregation. They took two of the four blocks in a dorm and used them for segregation. It was modified because there were like nine to eleven other people in there with you. You weren't in population, but you weren't in segregation either. It reminded me of when Mike, Nuke, and I caught the charge in the county. This was what they called punishment! More fights happened in modified segregation than in regular population. The regular segregation was so packed they were forced to take on another option. It was hot, and everyone wanted to go to the single-cell segregation to cool off. Just one of the things that occurred during the summer months on the youth spread.

I earned my G.E.D in 1997. I knew that they wouldn't have it on file at Polk, so I decided to sign up for the G.E.D program to

52

switch things up a little bit. I went to my case manager and asked her to enroll me in school. She told me she would and that the process would take about a week or two. One week later, I was in the block playing chess, talking junk to my opponent because I was beating him badly when an officer holding a paper called my name. He called one more and told us to pack our belongings because we were moving to the school dorm. I was excited because I would be getting my own room, which I hadn't had since my little kitchen stint a couple of months back.

Once I finished packing my belongings, I met with the officer in the hallway and he walked six other guys and myself to the yard. He radioed to the other officers that we were coming across the yard en route to the single cells. Upon my entrance into the building, I noticed how high everything was. When I entered the block, I was greeted by blank stares and a couple of dry what's ups. I found my room which was the twelfth room on the first floor. I put my things away, made my bunk like a pro, and then headed out to the block to see what was going on. I knew absolutely no one in my block, which was cool. If I hadn't learned anything, I learned how to rock solo and do me. I pulled up a chair and put my headphones in, so I could listen to the TV.

A guy pulled up a chair and said, "You from Wilson, ain'tcha?"

I wasn't sure if he was asking or telling me, but I replied, "Yeah. What made you ask that?"

"Well, most of you dudes are laid back with locks."

I chuckled because, for the most part, everyone had locks from Wilson at the time. We all were together in some way or another. Whether it was all of us on the yard, in a line, or at minimum two of us when we were not in the dorm. And I was the only one in a dorm by myself. If there was an issue with one, there was a peacemaker. And if we couldn't make peace, then we went to war, which was seldom done. The only time we rode as a unit was when Snott had a misunderstanding with a gang member about a porn book.

I will never forget it. It was the Heather Hunter issue of the *Black Video Illustrated*, which we just called "BVI." I wasn't sure how this was going to be handled because everything happened so fast. The guy had a slim to medium build, nothing intimidating. Rudeboy approached him and swung on him. He didn't get a clean hit, but it was good enough for the guy to be thrown off balance. He stumbled and Rodell got a clean shot, then he fell, only to spring back up like a sandbag clown. The guy swung as his life depended on it. He let loose a barrage of blows with his Walkman clutched in his fist. Before I realized, I'd been caught in the crossfire and he too was falling again. Then out of nowhere Snott landed the finishing blow. Just as fast as it started it was over.

We were lucky no officers saw it and that it didn't cause a lot of commotion. I got teased for a while about being the only one to get hit during the guy's barrage of blows. I was embarrassed about it because I was caught up in my feelings. I was able to see the humor in the whole ordeal later. The guy later sucker-punched a guy who was known to not fight back just so it would get him put in the hole for fighting. We called that a check-off move.

When my birthday came around, I had no clue how to spend it. I woke up early to go for breakfast. The first thing that came to my mind were the lyrics from the greatest MC ever, Nas, the song *Life's a Bitch* he and AZ recorded on Illmatic.

This was actually my second birthday incarcerated. I felt like I was shedding my youth and began to embody the characteristics of a man. I smoked a cigarette and took it all in. Where the fuck was I headed? What did I expect out of my bid? I thought to myself.

I went to the chow hall, ate, and kept my birthday to myself unless it was people who were in my circle. I found some weed on the camp later that day and smoked and thought about the streets. School for some reason crossed my mind.

I eventually grew tired of the GED program. I told the principal; once she confirmed my story, I was taken out of G.E.D. She asked me if I wanted to take some vocational classes to stay in school. I agreed to take the computer class and then take the industrial maintenance class afterward. Both of them were a joke. I enjoyed staying on gain time to keep my minimum at 2012 than 2016, but I learned absolutely nothing in any of the classes. We talked amongst ourselves and looked out the window and tried to figure which officer drove which car.

As fast as Wilson grew deep, we were quickly downsized. Rodell shipped out closer to home because he was getting closer to getting out. T.K, Raz, and Razor, all went home. Rudeboy shipped out and went to an adult spread because he was 21. It was time to start a new phase in my bidding process. I snuck down to the warehouse one morning with the warehouse workers. I had a plan, I needed some clippers in my hand. I needed to see the wizard, Mr. Brickle. He oversaw all the barbers and the warehouse.

Some of the warehouse workers relayed messages for me. I'd even written to him myself, but it was time to meet Mr. Brickle. I ran my spiel and he listened even though he already knew my intentions. He said the next barber spot to come open was mine. He sent me back to my dorm, but I didn't have anything to do so I asked if I could stay to help around the warehouse. He smiled and approved my request. I had nothing to do, and free time was my enemy at that point. So, I loaded supplies for the dorms and sent them out. We laughed and joked, which made time seem to fly. I won him over with my work ethic and calm demeanor.

Two weeks later a barber shipped out and I got the barber job in C-3, the work dorm. That meant I cut all the workers' hair. I didn't see the benefit then, but it allowed me to get paid twice. I got paid by the state and then I got paid canteen items from the guys. I must admit I was green at first and was being taken advantage of until another barber put me on to the game. From that point on, I could break my card and just live off the land. Just as in the streets the barber gets all of the news and knows what's going on. As it is on the outside, so is on the inside. I heard who was doing what, where the weed was, who broke into whose room, which officer was sneaking with which guy. It was crazy, I would see male officers beefing with an inmate because the inmate was having sex with a female officer that the officer liked. It was amazing how, the clippers and a cool personality would get guys to tell me all of their business.

Just as things started flowing smooth with the barber job, I found myself in a tight situation. Pride is worn on a sleeve and protected with every inch of your life, no matter who tests it—an inmate or an officer.

I was standing in line one day and an officer told me, "Shut the hell up."

I was talking and for some odd reason, they didn't want us talking while we were in line. I was wrong, I guess, but I couldn't live with the, "Shut the hell up!"

I responded back, "Fuck you!"

57

I was pulled out of line and asked to say what I said again.

I said, "what did you say to me?!"

He repeated it and so did I. I was taken to segregation for disrespecting and disobeying a direct order. I found myself in a place where I couldn't win. Around this time the state began to charge inmates $20 for each write up. I went to the hole, lost my job, and had to pay the fine. I lost all the way around but won with my pride.

Once I got out of the hole, I went to the dorms and settled in, but I wasn't content. I wanted to get back to the barbershop. The first chance I got, I snuck down to the warehouse and sat down with Mr. Brickle. He looked into the matter but had already given away my job. He promised me the next one that came open. He had been a man of his word thus far, so I expected him to hold true to his word. My part was done, so I just chilled in the dorms. I soon got caught up in the dorm culture of hustling and gambling. I almost forgot about trying to get back into the barbershop. Months went by and I was called to the sergeant's office and told to pack my shit because I was moving to C3. I was going back to the kitchen.

"What the hell? How in the world did they do this shit?" I thought.

I went to the kitchen and was terribly upset because I wanted my barber job. I didn't have shit to lose though, so I was willing to ride it out and see what happened.

I started off on the second shift for about two weeks. I wasn't feeling not having any time during the day to do anything, so I got switched to the first shift. That allowed me to have some time during the day to chill on the yard. My first day on first shift, Ms. Downing pulled me into her office and told me she wanted to give me a position in the stock room and in the coolers. She knew I didn't want to stay in the kitchen on pots and pans. She told me to just wait it out. When the position came open, I was put in the stock room.

The stockroom job was love, yet full of responsibilities. I had to keep track of what was being cooked throughout the week and pull certain meats out to defrost for later in the week. It was cool because it gave me perks. I ate what I wanted, smoked in the stock room, and hid from the staff from time to time. I actually began to enjoy my job because it was so laid-back. Just as I was getting used to my perks of being in the kitchen, it came to an abrupt end.

One morning, before Ms. Downing came in, the other officers were upset because they said we were doing too much talking. They threw mops, brooms, and squeegees on the floor and told us to grab one. Then they threw soap and water on the floor and told us to scrub. I complied, but after a while, it grew too redundant.

I told my man, Bino, "I'm out of here."

I dropped my broom and told the officers to lock me up. After they put me in handcuffs, I saw Bino do the same, and then a young dude, named Scrap. We were walked to our dorm and then to the hole. The officer who brought the papers for me to plead guilty, he told me that I was lucky. He said if one more person had followed my lead I would have been charged with inciting a riot. I ended up with a charge for disobeying a direct order and sentenced to ten days in segregation.

Once more I went to see Mr. Brickle in hopes of getting the next barber job. He kept his word and I got the job. I was assigned to C2, which was the school dorm. It wasn't much money, so my plan was to either get back to C3 or get across the yard in the dorms. The dorms had all types of crimes and hustles going on and I knew I could definitely get my weight up in the dorms. I made do with my current assignment because I was cool with the man who ran the outside canteen.

The outside canteen served both C2 and C3, as we shared the same yard, but were never outside together. It worked in my favor because I could tell the guys to leave my items in the canteen so I wouldn't have to traffic anything across the yard. It didn't work that well all the time, but it worked enough to keep the heat off me. The canteen man never charged me for any of the transactions because my haste helped fuel his hustle. He would charge them extra if they wanted to order more than the limited three items.

Outside of the usual canteen hustle, we were unknowingly tied into another little ring together. I wasn't huge on gambling, but I did take bets from time to time. Because I was back in the barbershop, I had a plethora of Newport cigarettes. It just so happened to be football season, so I began to take a couple of bets on some games. An officer overheard me and a guy make a bet one day. I didn't think much of it because I would make sure he didn't catch us handing over items. Sometime during the game, the officer pulled me to the side and asked me who I had my money on for the Steelers and Ravens game. I picked the Ravens and he said he'd bet me two packs. As I watched the game, I was pulling for the Ravens because I did actually have bets on them, regardless of what the officer had promised. Once the game was over and the Ravens pulled it off, the officer called me outside to get a mop bucket for the block.

In the mop closet, he handed me two packs of cigarettes. My face lit up because I didn't expect him to be any more than talk. Every week after that we would make our bets and paid each other whenever he worked in my dorm. We didn't keep a record of what we owed each other because we knew. How did this tie in with the canteen man? They had the same thing going on. While I would keep track of who owed who in my head, the canteen man had his bets written down in a notebook in his store, along with all the other people that owed him.

Out of the blue one day, I was called to the sergeant's office, handcuffed, and taken to the hole. They told me they had proof I was gambling with an officer and placed me under investigation. While in the hole, I heard they conducted a random inventory at all the canteens and found the canteen man's notebook. My name was in his book because he kept track of what I had left in there from cutting hair. What was so perplexing to me was they didn't lock up the canteen man. I ended up staying in the hole for thirty days due to reinvestigation.

Out of the hole and back in the dorms again. I just wanted to chill and get my thoughts together. I did, however, enjoy being able to go in my own room and chill. I had been on the camp for two years and a couple of months. I was growing tired of the "youth spread" (in North Carolina the prisons are also called spreads). Once more the Wizard came to get me and put the clippers back in my hand.

He told me, "Bullock, I don't know how such a smart young man like yourself end up in prison, let alone keep getting caught up in so much foolishness."

Mr. Brickle was always giving me some good words to ponder on. Although, I feel that he knew that his words ran through my ear as fast as they left his mouth. However, his words just as those from others that cared about me found a way to seep into my soul and were carried around unconsciously.

This time my job was to cut in the D-1 and D-2 dorms. I promised myself I would be careful in my walks this time and keep it on the straight and narrow. No sooner than I made this pact, I was met on the yard by the captain and lieutenant. They shook me down on my way back to my dorm from work. I had a couple of food items and some cigarettes on me. Since I didn't have a receipt for any of them, they confiscated everything except for my cigarettes since they were open and gave me a verbal warning.

Charging for haircuts was against policy. The rules were one haircut a month, no fades, and no facial trims unless you could submit a doctor's note. I broke all of the rules because it allowed me to hustle and save my money. I took heed to their warning; as far as for not having a receipt, I just made sure I had a long receipt when I walked across the yard. They never looked at the items when you had one. Some officers understood the hustle and as long as you gave them some cigarettes from time to time, they would let you bring the whole damn canteen across the yard. It was like paying a toll.

I started reading, which caused me to keep to myself more and more. I felt like all I did was smoke cigarettes, write letters, and read. Reading became my means of educating myself. I made it interesting and fun. When I ran across words that were foreign to me, I would write them down and beside them, I would write the page number. I would look up the word, go back, reread the sentence, and get a better understanding. That was how I began to build a vocabulary. Once I caught the reading bug, I was stuck. That was my escape and I used that tool to disappear on the regular. Sometimes I found I would become one with the book, dreaming about whatever setting I was reading. I'd wake up feeling crushed when I wasn't actually there.

Snott finished school and got a job as the third-shift janitor. He moved in the same block as me. This was cool because we always made sure that each other was straight. We wanted to start working out, but we smoked entirely too much weed and cigarettes, so we walked around the yard, hustled, and played middleman when we could.

One day, when we were coming in from off the yard, the officers turned the TV on. I thought it was odd because the TVs didn't usually come on until 2 o'clock. We all stood around, trying to figure out what the hell was going on.

A building was on fire. Minutes later, we saw another plane run into another building. The whole scene was chaotic. We all watched in awe as we saw people lose their lives on live television.

A news reporter eventually came on and said, "Each tower was struck with a plane that's hijacked."

We found out later that there was a third plane that made an attempt to hit the Pentagon. This day will forever be known as the infamous 9/11, which I found ironic since 911 was the number you called when there was an emergency. The officers wore faces of uncertainty over what was going to happen next. For the most part, "we" the live-in residents knew our next move…finish doing our time.

November 3rd was my grandmother's birthday which just so happened to fall on a Sunday, visitation day. I talked to my mom a couple of days earlier and they were going to come and see me. I was so excited to see my grandmother, I woke up early. I went to breakfast, washed up, put on my Sunday best, went to my room, and read, waiting for the officer in the booth to open my door for me to go to visitation. I ended up falling asleep and waking to the sound of chow call. I'd missed my visit.

I was so upset over not getting to see my grandma on her birthday that I only picked at my food and gave away my dessert. Once I got back to the block I played dominos with Snott and watched the *Larry Pickett Show*. Larry was like a local producer with a TV show from Raleigh. The second visit started and for some reason, the officer popped my door. I knew this was a mistake because they didn't play going to

65

another visitation time if you missed yours. If your visitor didn't come during your allotted time you were just out of luck. The officer then called my name over the intercom; once I made it to the door I was told to go to the chaplain's office. I took the long, clueless walk, trying to figure out what was going on. Once I walked in, I saw the chaplain, a short heavyset lady with an afro. She greeted me and offered me a seat, which I accepted. She began to speak as a mother would to her child.

She took my hand and said, "I understand that you were supposed to get a visit today, and today is your grandmother's birthday."

"Yes, ma'am," I responded.

"I heard that you two have a good relationship, and you stayed with her for quite a while." I nodded my head in agreement. "Well, when your mom and sister were going to pick your grandmother up to come to see you, they found that she had passed away."

It felt like I had swallowed a golf ball. She had just knocked the wind out of me, a gutshot from VinnyTyson. She picked up the phone and called my mom. Once I heard my mom's voice, I could breathe again and my voice came back. We talked for a while and she told me that she would come to see me soon. Once I was done on the phone, I stood and turned for the door.

The chaplain said as if she was speaking with a heavy heart, "Ronald you wouldn't be allowed to go to the funeral, but I will grant you a special visit."

I nodded my head to assure her that I understood, thanked her, and exited her office. Just as clueless as I had walked to the chaplain's office, I walked back to the dorm. When I got back to the dorm, the dayroom was still full. I went to tell Snott what was going on and then went to my room, so I could smoke and think.

The following week was long, I had no idea what my family was going through; however, I did know that all of my family was at the big house. The chaplain held true to her word and allowed me to get a special visit. My parents and my aunt Jackie, my mom's sister, came to see me a couple of days before the funeral. We talked about everything, yet nothing in particular. They told me that the funeral was set for the 11th, which just so happened to be my birthday. I started a yearly ritual from that birthday forward. I would fast on both the 3rd and the 11th of every November.

A little before thanksgiving, the camp sent out a Christmas package list for each person to fill out and send to their families, with hopes of receiving something. The list consisted of snacks and other foods that weren't sold on the normal prison canteens. This was big. Even if you had no idea of Christmas, you were definitely going to take advantage of this opportunity. Everyone found them a cooking partner around this time and ordered things together. We didn't have a microwave at Polk, so we had to take this into consideration when we made our orders. Once we sent them off, the anticipation began.

It seemed as if time dragged as we waited on the boxes to be delivered. Because I was on the Brickle team, I had the privilege of unloading and passing out the boxes. It was cool to see the guys' faces when they opened their boxes and completely the opposite when guys thought they got one but didn't.

That year the packages arrived on a Friday. Snott and I set out on the mission to find some weed to go along with our packages. And as always, we completed the mission. On Saturday night when the college hip-hop station "straight from the crate" came on we decided that we would lock ourselves in a room and listen to the radio and just "blow." Just as soon as I lit the joint up, Jay-Z's new song, *Song Cry*, pierced our eardrums and we were stuck.

Snott said that his little brother was just telling him about that song. As if the DJ read my mind, he ran the song back, and by the time the joint was over, the song ended and I found myself listening to it once more on my mental playback. I don't think that I heard another song after that. What I did hear next was trouble. The dorm door slid open and a lady's voice said, "Pop D-201!"

Snott and I looked at each other with a face of conviction. We knew the consequences of our actions, so we lit up cigarettes and smoked. When the officer came in she was hysterical.

"What the fuck are you two doing in here?" she yelled.

Snott always being a smart ass, replied, "Just smoking and talking."

Our eyes were crimson red. She closed the door and locked us back in. We couldn't let them get the evidence, so we smoked it! When she came back she had the sergeant and the lieutenant. They took me to my room and made me pack my property and Snott did the same. Once again, my decisions lead me back to segregation.

I didn't know when they were coming to do a drug test on me, but I knew it was soon, so I drank water all day every day. That water was nasty. It was hard, plain horrific, but like everything else in prison I adapted to it. When they did come two weeks later, I produced the clearest urine I've ever seen. From the time the officer left with my sample, I prayed and hoped that it would test clean. One day while waiting on my lunch tray to come, Mr. Brickle popped up and talked to me for a long time.

What really stuck in my mind was, "Bullock, you can't continue to dig a ditch then jump in and keep expecting help out of the ditch. I can't help you out of this one!"

His words sank in my soul and weighed on me. I knew this one was out of his hands. I had made my own bed, so I laid in it. The lieutenant came another two weeks later and said that my test was negative. I just had to plea to a couple of lesser charges of being in an unauthorized area, for which I had already served my time. Christmas had passed, and it was a couple of days before New Year's, so it was refreshing to spend that on the yard. When I got out, I was looking for Snott, but he was still in the hole. He later told me that he tampered with his test because he knew he was dirty. He ended up doing forty-five days before he was released.

Once again, I found myself in the dorms and felt as if the Wizard had pulled his last magic trick for me, so I didn't ask about a job. I was a bit embarrassed to even ask him for any more assistance since he laid his good words on me. I stayed in the dorms and chilled, returned to my normal loaning and middle-manning deals to get by. Then just as always, a barber job came open and I found it impossible to sit it out. I didn't have the gall to ask Mr. Brickle for another shot, so I sent a letter by the canteen man. In my letter, I apologized and told him how much his words meant and how I was willing to do right. Once more, he believed in me and took another chance on me.

When I move to the single-cell I was met at the door by Snott. That was one hell of a surprise. He got the job as a segregation janitor. The dorm that I was assigned to cut was the dorms that I just left, D3-D4. Just as soon as I picked up the clippers I began to get my hustle on. I felt that my time was limited on the camp since I was twenty-one, so all I wanted to collect was cigarettes and stamps. The two were literally prison currency. Not even a good month after getting my barber job my gut feeling was on point. After leaving the barbershop for the day, I went to the yard to kick it with some of the fellas. Just as soon as I reached the yard about everyone that I saw told me that Snott and J.B. were looking for me. I found the two walking around together.

"Man, we shipping out in the morning," J.B. said.

"We who?" I shot back.

"You, me, Gizmo, and two more dudes.'

They told me that they got the word from a guy who worked in the administration office, so it was official. Snott didn't say much at the time, but J.B. said that we were going to Pasquotank. After he said his piece, he walked away, and Snott and I walked laps around the yard until it closed. After two years and approximately four months at Polk Youth Institution, I was on my way to the adult spread. That night

Snott and I talked until lockdown. It was a bittersweet moment, like losing a brother.

Chapter 3

GROWN MAN BUSINESS

After waking up at 4 a.m. I couldn't imagine that I had a three-hour ride ahead of me. This was a Monday ship so this was considered a special ship out. When I saw everyone who was shipping I knew that it was only to make room for an incoming transfer. J.B., Gizzmo, two white guys, one called himself crazy and the other guy named David who no one had ever seen on the yard, and myself. None of us were trouble-makers, but we weren't model inmates either.

Crazy was the only one who was gang-related. That was a topic that was discussed among the four of us on the ride. J.B., Gizzmo, and I told him to lay his flag down before we even arrived at Pasquotank. He said that he was good and grown and could handle himself. However, we all knew that he wasn't too good at that, from his history of fighting. He was right about one thing though, he was good and grown. Anyway, the three of us vowed that we would keep up with each other as long as no one got into anything crazy. It's amazing how riding in a vehicle can cause you to cramp up and just feel uncomfortable, after going a period without riding. Not to mention that you are shackled, handcuffed, and have a waist chain on to connect the two. We all talked for about an hour. Besides sleeping, I found myself contemplating where I was headed and what my game plan was.

Hours passed and we were finally coming up on our destination. Seeing the concrete warehouse rising from the shadows of the trees caused our anxiety to rise. The stillness of the air spoke volumes. The guard who was driving cut through the awkward vibe with words of advice.

"This is just a bigger Polk. The same way you handled yourself there, do here. Stay out of the bullshit and the bullshit will not come to find you. Fight if you have to and you three are pretty good guys so keep doing what ya'll do and you will be just fine. As for you," he said, referring to Crazy because no one had addressed David the entire ride, who seemed to be in his own little world, "you will find out who the real gangsters are. If you don't stop that silly shit, you will make your sentence longer and harder than it is or should be!"

After he finished trying to somewhat comfort us, he went back into C.O. mode. When we arrived, it was definitely apparent that we weren't at Polk anymore. It felt like being dropped off in the neighboring city's hood, where you weren't sure if you knew anyone. However, you were sure that there was some common ground, so you could make it work. When we pulled up into receiving, I noticed that there were three yards, all divided by fences. All three of the yards were big in comparison to where we just left and all three were occupied at the time. Guys working out, playing basketball, horseshoes, and as always you can tell who was hustling. We pulled all the way into the port where we were to get out and get processed.

Once we entered the processing area, we were told to strip butt naked as if we were arriving on the shores of Charleston, South Carolina and appraised for auction. This time we didn't have to shower. The four officers there gave us some more boxers and asked us for our clothes sizes. We were given a set of browns and then they gave us our dorm location.

One of the officers said, "We didn't check your personal bags because, if you have any contraband, either someone will take that from you or our snitches will tell us."

When we were given our housing location, Gizzmo, J.B., and Crazy went to Unit 4, I went to Unit 2, and David went to Unit 3. Unit 1 was for segregation. Once we got our assignments, we headed down the tunnel, which was patrolled by one of the several guards who were stationed in the booths and at certain doors. They helped guide me to my unit, dorm, and then my room. When I was going up; I heard my name called.

I turned around and saw my man Black from Goldsboro. We use to kick it at Polk. Black was definitely aware of what was going on in the yard so we had to link up. I told him where I was being housed and he said that he would come up. Once I reached my dorm, I stopped to talk to the guy in the booth, and let him know what room I was in. I'll never forget it, eleven down.

There were sixteen rooms on each floor, an odd side and an even side. Downstairs was down and upstairs was up. When I entered the dorm, what I saw spooked me and will always be etched in my brain. There was a big, tall, heavy-set guy with long hair, no facial hair, stretching his legs. He was doing a standing up split. One of his legs was touching the shower wall and the other one firmly planted on the floor. He saw me and nodded; I nodded back. I just hoped I wasn't his type because I wasn't quite sure I could take him. That thought made me fully realize, I was now in the penitentiary.

I went into my cell and just as I started unpacking, Black made his way up to my room. After witnessing that, I needed to smoke like ASAP. Black came in and we talked and smoked.

I didn't finish unpacking, because they made a yard call, and we went outside.

Outside, we linked up with a couple of guys that we knew from Polk. Black was called to his case manager's office, so he left the yard. I kicked it with A.D., Beretta, Gizzmo, and J.B. We talked about Polk, all that we were into, and who was doing what. There was another yard call, so if you wanted to go in or missed the first yard call to go out. I stayed out and had a smoke as I walked around to the basketball court, to the Unit 3 fence, and back to the Unit 4 fence. I was looking for someone from Wilson.

Lo and behold, when I reached the Unit 4 fence I saw Dre, CLIP, and Shawn. We talked about who we knew, where we hung out, what side of town we stayed on, all the people who we knew in common, and so on and so forth. We also talked about who we ran across on state and who was where and how much time they had. It was catch-up, homeboy talk. Dre and I went to elementary school together, so we caught up on the old days. While we were talking, he put me up on what was going on around the yard, who was who, and what was what. He said that he just came up for his medium custody, so he was looking to ship out soon if he made it. The yard finally closed and it was time to go in and get ready for chow time.

When I got back in the block, I went to my room, started unpacking and getting everything in order. I heard a knock on my door and saw a short, brown-skinned, bald-headed older guy who looked to be around his late thirties or early forties. My door was closed and locked because that was the rule at Polk. He asked me where I had transferred from. I guess he was part of the welcoming council of the block. I told him to get my door popped so we could talk face to face. He did and then introduced himself as Philly. I shook his hand and looked him dead in the eye. I couldn't show any signs of weakness because I didn't know his intentions nor those of any of the onlookers. Although I wasn't sure who was paying attention, I'm sure there were eyes on the new young guy.

I cut our conversation short because I didn't want to seem as if I was pressed to make any acquaintances. I didn't lock my door this time as I went back to getting my things together. I told him I would holla at him later. When I got into a groove in organizing my room, they called chow. I walked out and followed the crowd to the cafeteria. I saw quite a few people stop at a booth on the right side of the tunnel. It registered that they were going to med call before going to eat. Through the tunnel from my block to the chow hall, I know there were at least six officers that would randomly call someone to the side and do a pat-down. It caused me to put this prison thing in proper perspective. If they were doing random pat-downs going into the chow hall, they were looking for a shank or some other paraphernalia. I knew I was on the "Spread" then.

I walked in the chow hall and there were two officers and a control booth who looked down on the whole room. I didn't know which line to get in and I assumed that it really didn't matter. The last thing I wanted to do was to look lost and vulnerable. That's like an open wound in the ocean—the sharks can sense it miles away. I was in line behind a big, bald-headed black guy. At that point, I wanted to know if the bald head was really a prison thing. But I guessed they had worried themselves bald, or gray.

The dude turned around and said, "What's up Rap. I'm Willie." We shook hands and I looked him square in the eye. "So where are you from?" he asked.

"Wide-A-Wake Wilson," I said proudly because I knew for the most part dudes from Wilson held their own well on state. I asked where he was from.

"The Queen City, Charlotte," he said with a chuckle. I chuckled too because I knew he was trying to match my intensity. "Man I got a partner from Wilson that I went to job corp. with back in the day," Willie said.

We paused our conversation when we reached the window to get our trays. The windows that were covered with a white vinyl material that hid the kitchen workers. He got his tray and I got my no meat substitute meal because I was hungry. I followed him to get the drinks and then to the table. It was self-defeating to try to hold a conversation while going through this because in between talking to the kitchen workers and staff and other people, a conversation was impossible. When we sat down and picked up where we left off.

"Hit Man! His name is Hit Man Higgs," Willie continued.

"Hell yeah, I know Robert. That's my people. He is damn near family."

"Shit I got a picture of him in the dorm," I said.

"If that's your people, you my people, youngin' you good around here."

It's crazy how small the world is. "Lil Wilson, when I say that he earned his name, he was serious with his hands, and a solid dude," he added.

I was glad that I came up under good solid dudes who held it down wherever they went. Just as Robert had left a good name for himself, that reputation was extended for Wilson dudes who came after him. I planned on doing the same for myself and the guys who came after me. We continued to talk about everything while we ate, although he did the majority of the talking about when he and Hit Man were in job corps. It was cool with me. I've never been a big talker anyway. After we finished eating we walked back to the dorm, and just to solidify my word. I showed Willie the picture of Hit-Man that my man Stank had sent me just a couple of months ago.

He invited me up to his room and we kicked it. He put me up on game as far as who was who, what was what, what he was into, and what was happening on Unit 2. I told him that I was a barber and wanted to get into the barbershop when a spot came open. After that, I went to my room to smoke because Willie didn't smoke or even allow anyone to smoke in his room. It was getting late anyway so I told him that I would kick it with him the next day.

I was called to my case manager's office the following week. When I reached the office in which I was directed to I noticed it was empty. I stood outside until I was given further directions. While I was waiting, I saw a short, petite lady headed in my direction. My god, was she beautiful.

"Ronald Bullock?" she said in a reassuring tone.

"Yes." I'm not sure how I was able to muster that little bit out. Never in my life had I been intimidated by a woman's beauty. I figured my incarceration had affected me in more ways than I thought. She entered first and invited me in. She introduced herself as Ms. Perry. I shook her hand and took my seat.

"Sir, I didn't ask you to have a seat!" she snapped. I stood back up and apologized. "When you enter someone's office, you should never sit until asked!"

Her scolding embarrassed me, so I apologized again. If I wasn't already uneasy by her looks, her reprimand made it worse.

"Ok, Mr. Bullock, please have a seat," she said with a grin.

I sat and she asked me what were my plans and goals for the duration of my stay at Pasquotank Correctional Institution? That was a hell of a question because I didn't have the slightest idea. All I knew was that I wanted to cut hair. I told her the first thing that came to my mind. I know that she sensed youthful bullshit. I did, however, let it be known that I wanted the barber job once there was an opening. She said that there weren't any openings at that time, but I had to do something, and there were kitchen jobs open at the moment. I chuckled and told her I had a bad record in the kitchen so I wasn't sure if that was a good move for me.

"Well you do know that you are on an adult camp now, so you beating little boys up isn't a concern here!" I smiled and realized that she had my transcript open on her computer. "Oh, and you can definitely forget getting others to walk out of the kitchen with you!"

"They always make things sound worse than they actually are," I said. I knew from the tone of this conversation, I was going to work in the kitchen, as a way of her showing me her authority. "What about my hours as a barber, does that not count for anything?"

"Oh, yes. When we need a barber on the unit I will remember you, but as for right now we need kitchen workers."

She said I would have a custody review coming up in November, and if I kept my nose clean I would be in medium custody, and out of the kitchen. She chuckled and then dismissed me.

When I got back to the unit, I decided to hit the yard for a while and kick it with my homeboys. Just as soon as I got on the yard, I saw Dre. He said that he just came up for medium custody, so he was a little excited. Me coming up for my medium custody in November was best thing that came out of the meeting that I had with Ms. Perry.

I told him about my new dilemma with going to the kitchen and somehow we found humor in it, considering my history in the kitchen. I asked where CLIP and Shawn were. He said CLIP was in the dorm and Shawn was at work in the gym. Shawn and Dre were third-shift janitors; however, Shawn just got on in the gym, which was more money and less stressful. The gym job was one of the best jobs to have in prison. It was ranked up there with the canteen job and the barber job. The gym job had a lot of perks. They set up for just about every event that went on in the prison and basically had access to every dorm, and therefore, access to everyone in regular population. It went without saying that the gym worker had to be well respected by his peers as well as staff. I guess we all had something to look forward to in some way or another.

I was rereading my last personal book, *The Mis-Education of the Negro* by Carter G. Woodson, for the second time. While laid back on my bunk, I got lost in his perspective of what it is to be a black person, educated in the euro-centric school system. I was snapped back to another harsh reality. I heard a small voice yelling library call and a deeper voice echoing behind. I place a bookmarker in between the pages and stepped out to see how long before the last call. The officer said that it would be in five minutes, which gave me time to step back in my room, put my shoes on and grab my ID card.

There weren't many people from my dorm going to the library. There was a tall, slim guy in line who I'd never seen in the block. My mind began to wander because I'd seen things like this play out in so many different ways, so I kept my distance and stayed on guard. It could be a hit. He could be a thief, waiting to break into a room, or he could be leaving his penitentiary lover's room. It's crazy how in just a few flips of the calendar, your entire perspective of life and survival can change. The reality that you once knew becomes warped and irrelevant.

As the doors began to slide open, I saw Willie entering. His eyes grew wider when he saw the slim guy. It seemed as if he was excited to see him and vice versa. "Damn Wise, they hid yo' ass didn't they?"

They walked hard and fast toward each other. When they finally got within arms' reach, they shook hands and embraced as if it had been ages since they last saw each other. I took it that Wise had just gotten out of the hole. The door opened again and this was the final call, so Wise told Willie that he would get with him once he came back from the library. Wise, two other guys, and I filed out of the dorm and were radioed to the library.

I was a little unsure of where to go, so I followed the rest of the guys. As we were walking down the tunnel, it seemed as if everyone called out to Wise or acknowledged him, residents and staff alike. It was clear how popular he was.

Once we started up the stairwell he said, "Peace young God," stuck out his hand and said, "Wise."

"Peace," I replied. "Udy."

"You seem to be very observant and cautious. I peeped that from the dorm. I respect that."

"Thanks. I'd rather be cautious than sorry."

"I understand that? You did say your name was Udy, right? Did I pronounce it correctly?"

"Yes, and you are one of the few that got it right on the first try!"

We chuckled. He asked me what it meant and what my nationality was. I told him it was a name my mother had given me as a baby and that I was black.

"I've never heard it before, but I do want to let you know that you are not black, and we can build on that later."

"Bet." I said. He then asked me what camp I came from because he hadn't seen me around prior to him going to the hole. "I came from Polk a couple of weeks ago."

He said I seemed a little mature to be coming fresh off the youth spread. We approached the library, where we were patted down at the door and walked through metal detectors. I didn't know if we needed special clearance to get in. I damn sure felt secure in there, with all of the security.

I headed toward the African American section and Wise beelined toward the reference section. I was looking for Langston Hughes, James Baldwin, or Richard Wright. I looked around after I found a book of Langston Hughes's short stories. I figured that would keep me occupied for a while. They allowed you to check out magazines, so I took full advantage of that opportunity. You could only check out one at a time and there was a two-day limit on them. I suppose they put such a short limit on it to allow everyone the chance to see them before the next one came out.

I walked past the tables and saw Wise was deeply submerged in an American History book. He was writing

86

vigorously in a notebook, while glancing back a smaller book on his left side which had a blue circle and a red 7 in the center. That little book looked as if it had really been used because the cover was badly worn and holding on for dear life.

After about an hour or so, the guard who had patted us down stood up and said, "Unit two, you all have about five minutes to go ahead and check your books out and put the reference books away and line up at the door."

I was about ready to leave anyway. I had become restless and ready to get back to the block and possibly go outside. On our way out, we were patted down again. Since not a lot of people were in line, it wasn't hard for Wise to find me.

On our way out the door, he asked me, "What is your belief system?"

I felt like this was a trick question coming from him, but I could only answer with a truthful answer. Instead of giving him a direct answer, I gave him the long version to show a little diversity.

"I was raised Christian. I've studied the 5 percenter Nation of God's and Earth's. I go to Jummah on Friday and Taaleem on Tuesday, but I'm also leaning toward Rastafari at this point."

He said, "Damn you want it all at one time, huh?"

"Nah I just want to get my own perspective of life."

"Well, what's your understanding of all of these things?"

"I respect all religions. I don't agree with everything, but in all due respect, I take out what applies to me and apply the principles to my life."

"Indeed so," he agreed.

I then asked him was he, GOD? I assumed that he was part of the 5 percenter Nation, as the attribute Wise was a common name within the movement. He said that he was now a member of the Moorish Science Temple. I've never heard of this so I asked him to break it down for me. He said that he would build with me on that later because it took some time, but with the free mind that I had I would be able to understand it.

We talked about our time at Polk and how things had changed since he was there. When we reached the block we saw Willie.

"I see you two have met," Willie said. "That's cool. Lil Wilson, Wise is a good dude for you to know."

"I see," I said.

Willie told Wise and me that he had something for us after the count time following last chow call. I wasn't sure what he had for us because he had his hands in some of everything. When they called chow, Wise waited on me so we could walk together. He then began to call names, some of which I knew, some I knew of, and others I had never heard of a day in my life. Going through the tunnel, a guard stopped me and pulled me to the side to give me a pat-down and then told me to move along. I caught back up with Wise and we picked up where we left off.

We went into the chow hall and a couple of his homeboys came and stood with us in line. Wise introduced the three of us to each other. They were all from little Washington and the Plymouth area. We all sat down at a table and they asked me where my meat was. It was a question I'd grown accustomed to hearing and one that I'd grown creative in answering over the years.

I let them know that I'd been a vegetarian since 1999 and that I had no plan on breaking that habit anytime soon because state meat looked horrible. They laughed and said I was disciplined and that they were trying to do the same thing.

I found out that their laughs were sarcastic. They were laughing because I said 1999 like it was a long time ago. They had all been locked up for between five and eight years.

I chuckled and said, "Shit. That's still a long time not to eat meat."

"Calm down youngin. We only joking. Shit!" one of Wise's homeboys said.

"My man is from Wilson," Wise piped in.

"I went to barber school with a guy from Plymouth," I offered and told them who I knew from down that way.

We talked about them and then my homeboys who they knew. Wise invited all of us to the Moorish Science Temple that Friday. I accepted his invitation. I didn't know any Muslims there yet, so I didn't want to go to Jummah.

After chow, on our way to our units, one of the guards pulled me to the side and patted me down again. This time I grew a little frustrated, tightening my body when the officer touched me hoping that he could sense my frustration. I asked Wise how common was it for them to get you twice. He said they were just messing with me because I was new. I had never been good when I was being picked on and hoped it would end soon.

When I got back to my room, it had been ransacked. No one was sitting in the dayroom that I could ask. I looked for all my valuables and found they were still there. I hollered at Wise and told him what happened.

He laughed and said, "Damn. Today just isn't your day, huh?" He said they searched rooms there without you being present.

"Well, damn," I said. "Why are they fucking with me today?"

Once I get my room back in order, a short, slim, balding officer came to my door and said, "I searched your room earlier. Everything is good."

"Damn. Why do ya'll do shit like that? I'm glad I had someone to tell me that's what ya'll do, or I would've been left to assume some wrong shit."

"Well, it's a good thing that you didn't assume anything because I would hate to pull someone off your little young ass!" he said, in a matter-of-fact tone.

They called count after chow and the yard closed for the day. I went to my room and prepared for a shower. Willie told me once I get out of the shower to go holla at Wise. I hit all of the hot spots and ran the water through my newly formed dreads, and got out of there. I put on my clothes and grabbed my cigarettes. Since I still didn't know everyone in the block, I kept my sneakers on just to be on the safe side.

Wise was chilling on the top tier in front of his room. When he saw me, he motioned for me to come up and told me to bring some Newports. When I went up to his room, he put up his curtain over the window on his door and damped a towel and put it at the bottom of the door and then lit an incense. He took a wood-tip cigar and split it in half and dumped it in a wad of tissue and flushed the contents. He then poured the weed in the split cigar. Once he finished rolling the blunt, he gave me the honors of lighting it up and starting the cipher.

The local college, Elizabeth State University, had a radio station that was playing rap music from the mid-90s. The whole scene played out like some old damn prison movie, yet at the same time, some time-travel shit. With the music and the weed, I actually felt like I was in the streets once again. Nas and Noreaga's song *Body in the Trunk* poured through the makeshift sound system made of Styrofoam cups and some pro 35 headphones. The dimmed lights and the music allowed me to mentally hit the fence and go back to Wilson and chill at the dead-end sign on Coleman Street.

In that moment, I admonished myself for my lack of good judgment in the past. I totally forgot that Wise was in the room until he snapped out of his trance and began to speak.

"Yo, you do know and understand that we are not black. Right?"

I wasn't sure if I was ready to come back to prison at that point so I acted as if I didn't hear him. It was a topic that I wanted to build upon, but just not then. I guess he understood my state of mind because he didn't try to jar my attention. He sat back and picked up where he initially left off on his zone.

I lit another cigarette to boost my high. As I smoked, I relived entering the dreadful gates of the penitentiary in slow motion. Wise busted another wood-tip cigar and filled it with weed. I needed this vehicle to transport me one more time. This time as he rolled the toothpick-sized blunt. He knew that he had my attention and proceeded to capitalize on the opportunity. He asked for a short on the cigarette, but it was too good to give a short so I just gave him a whole one.

"So Udy, what is your nationality?" he asked.

"I'm African. My ancestors were stolen and given a false identity and therefore my duty is to find my identity."

"Well you are not completely wrong and neither are you totally right, but that is a cool answer."

"America is the most bastardized nation in the world. There is nothing originally from here. The language is English and the flag is a hoax, but they have one."

I guess he saw the confusion on my face because he attempted to clarify things. He cracked a smile and added on.

"See every nation of people has a flag that represents them, and many will go to war for their flag. Our people were born here but we are not a part of this country, we are not represented in the constitution nor any of its amendments. If you read the Dread Scott case of 1857 you will see that we are, still not citizens of this county."

Finally, he lit the blunt and took two deep pulls. He looked into the air as if he had inhaled wisdom from a past spirit. He passed me the blunt and picked up his lesson.

"To give you a brief description and understanding of what I'm saying, "they" call us black and call themselves white, which is just a play on words, but concerning the so-called black people, is there a flag for black people?"

I thought about it for a while and then responded, "Yes. There are a few flags for the so-called black people. There is the black panther flag, the black liberation, the nation of Islam, and the nation of Gods and Earths. All of them have a flag."

I felt as if I had made one hell of an argument. He gave a mean chuckle and said, "once again you are not all the way wrong. These are flags, but they are flags for movements and do not represent the body. They cannot be taken to represent a nation amongst the United Nations. You also made mention of you being an African. Well, once again youngin', you are wrong. You do know that Africa is a continent and not a country and there is no one flag for an entire continent?"

I took a long pull and absorbed the information. It all made sense and was actually something I could research myself. And I very well planned to.

"Now tell me if black is your nationality," he said.

The blunt was gone. It took me on a journey far different than the first one I had. I was lost in thoughts about a history of lies. It was about to be count time so I dapped him up and went to my room. I laid down and continued to ponder on the information.

I was on the yard talking to CLIP and Dre about our next move and Dre told me that he was expecting to ship out soon because he just made his medium custody. CLIP was waiting to get a response back on his custody review. During our conversation I was paged to the dorm.

I went to the officer on the yard and told them that I had been called to the dorm. He walked me in and rerouted me to the side door of the kitchen. Two others were standing and talking when I arrived. The officer in the control booth paged the kitchen supervisor. A short, gray-haired white guy came to the door and let us in.

"Follow me so you can sign these papers," he said.

He didn't introduce himself or anything. I found that rude, but understood his coldness. He gave us each a thin stack of papers and told us to read them if we wanted to or we could just sign them and save him time. We later found out that everyone called him Mr. O because no one could pronounce his name. He went into his office and sent Mr. Watson to give us a full tour of the kitchen. Afterward, he gave each of us our shift assignment and white pants. We'd just been assigned to kitchen duty.

I was assigned second shift in the dish room. My duties consisted of dumping the remaining food from the trays into the trash can and loading them into the dishwasher. After all of the dorms had eaten and all the trays were cleaned, I helped sweep and mop the floors. After that, I was allowed to go to the dorm for the night.

I dreaded being in the kitchen during the day around all the stinking ass food, not to mention the guys that took pride in cooking the nasty food, as if they really put a spin on it and made it better. Not all but some guys, mainly the cooks, acted as if they were irreplaceable like they were part inmate, part correctional officer because they got a dollar a day. With my past experience of the silly dudes throwing their trays in the window, and the guys in segregation literally putting shit in their trays because of boredom. I had to get out of the kitchen, like soon.

I decided my next move would be to go to my case manager's office to see if there were any barber jobs open or coming open soon. The next morning I made my move to see Ms. Perry unannounced.

When I knocked on the door and she saw my face, she said, "Bullock, I didn't call you in today."

"I know Ms. Perry, but I really need you bad!"

"No, Mr. Bullock, you need to put in your request to see me."

"Just give me a few minutes."

"I'm cutting my break short. Talk fast!" she said.

"Look, I gotta get out of the kitchen before I end up in segregation. Is there a barber job open anywhere on the compound?"

She broke out a big smile and said, "What have you heard?"

Actually I hadn't heard anything, but I knew that there was something by her body language, so I played along. "Something is supposed to be open soon. I'm not sure which unit, but I just wanted to be considered when the position comes open!"

I knew I had just hit the jackpot on pure luck. She said that she would look up my hours as a barber since I'd been on state, then dismissed me. I had snuck to her office illegally, but I left legally and with a little hope.

It was time to go to work and I really hated going in more than anything, since my newfound hope. Entering the side door, Mr. Watson did his normal pat-down and roll call for the second shift. We were allowed to eat lunch before the regular population. I sat with a dude named Phil, he was cool for the most part. I saw him in the kitchen and he seemed to have a little pull, which was a little odd since he wasn't a cook. We talked about our home towns and who we knew from each other's city. He gave me some tips on how to make my job a little easier.

He told me that Mr. Watson was cool and didn't give a damn what we ate as long as it didn't affect the population and we didn't take any food back to the block. After we went back to our work stations and began our daily duties, I took Phil's advice and looked busy in front of Mr. O. I made sure all the garbage cans were empty so I could chill after that. After Mr. O left, I went to the dining area, smoked a cigarette, and talked to a couple of guys who were smoking. Once my break was over I slid to the back, mopped the floor, and then headed toward the restroom.

When I turned the knob, the door was locked, so I left. I didn't have to go that bad anyway. I started looking for Phil because I wanted to ask him if he knew someone that I was on the youth spread with. I searched every cut and hiding spot I knew of and asked everyone. The reaction I got from most of everyone was awkward, as if they knew something I should have known.

A guy they called Trey-four pulled me to the side and told me that dude had a boy in the restroom. He then apologized to me for not telling me earlier. From that point on, I was skeptical about what I ate in the chow hall. That incident put me really over being in the kitchen. To add to my drama, when I got off work that day, the officer gives me my mail and a relocation slip. I was moving to the kitchen block. How bad of a day could this be?

I had grown accustomed to everyone in the dorm. They all looked at me like the little brother of the block. Wise came to my door and asked if I needed some help. I accepted the offer. Somewhere in the middle of my relocating, I was called

98

to the sergeant's office. Really not in the mood for any more bad news, I looked to the sky and asked for strength. When I reached the door, there's a tall, dark-skinned guy with an old school, box haircut. I smirk and he returns a chuckle. He looked like he was stuck in the late eighties, early nineties era with that haircut. He chuckled that I had to move all my things back to my old block.

"You're Bullock, right?" he asked.

"Yes, sir."

"Well, I know that you are in the middle of moving, but we need for you to move your things back to your original block."

"Why? What's up?" I'm extremely aggravated at this point.

"Young man, I see that you just came from Polk. Damn sho' hope you can cut some hair, 'cause dey put you in the barbershop."

Damn. Ms. Perry worked pretty fast. I thanked old school for the information and then went back into the block to tell Wise that we moved for nothing! I smoked a cigarette and got my thoughts together, putting everything away again. Once everything was back in place and I smoked a cigarette, I told Wise I wasn't smoking weed anymore. I had worked too hard to get out of the kitchen to get a dirty urine test and start back all over again. I took a shower and tried to get some rest for the next day, but I already knew that sleep would be evasive. I listened to the quiet storm, smoked a couple of cigarettes, and let sleep eventually find me.

The very next day I hit the yard, looking for the barber that I would be working with. The search was quicker than I imagined. Everyone on the yard knew Reid and, rightfully so, he was a cool guy. I approached him once I found out who I was looking for. I was kind of apprehensive at first because the environment on the yard at this point was awkward tension between "old heads" and "young bucks."

The "old heads" thought that the "young bucks" were disrespectful, and we were changing the code of doing time. This I could have learned on only the adult spread, being among guys who have seen the evolution of prison. I'm sure that the "old heads" before them thought the same. But this was a new wave with the gang activities.

As I walked in his direction, he stuck his hand out and said, "Congrats and thanks all at the same damn time. I'm Reid. When I found out they had replaced the other barber, I began asking around too."

We talked for a while, we asked each other the normal icebreaking questions, and then he hit me with one that I'm sure I was asked over a million times during the course of the next month or so. "How long have you been cutting?"

I answered the question the same way every time. Not being too direct, yet inserting the information that I knew would be holding their attention. "I've been cutting a while, but I finished barber school in '98."

That response always lead to other questions. "Where did you go to school?" "How long you been locked up?" "You had some dope didn't you?", and the list goes on. He told me that he would give me the rundown on the do's and don'ts and how I was in a winning situation. He told me a piece of vital information that I definitely took heed to.

"It's a lot of snitching, hating ass dudes around here. I don't know what you do, but keep your nose clean until everyone gets to know you. Some people are mad 'cause you got the job and you just got here."

Once we parted ways, I headed to my room so I could go through my things to make sure I had no contraband in my room. I also drank water like I worked out in a desert. The water was the only way that I knew to try to clean my system. By no means did I want to lose my barber job already by smoking weed.

On my first day on the job, I was kind of nervous because I had no idea what to expect. I was used to cutting all levels of dudes on the youth spread, from the pretty boy dudes that were trying to pull a female staff member to the new guys processing. I never questioned my barber skills. I just didn't know what type of people I would be dealing with. I kicked it with Reid for a minute while we prepared to open the shop.

He told me plain and simple, "Just cut the best that you can, and if they don't like it, fuck em'. Make sure they pay you and you will be straight. You won't have to click your card no more."

We kicked it a little more, and then all of a sudden an officer came in. She told us she was going to pass out the barber list to the assigned dorm and return it to us so that we could get started.

Reid cut two heads before anyone would sit in my chair. My very first client was an older guy who worked in the kitchen. He wanted a low-even all over because he was thinning. During the haircut, I broke the ice. I asked where he was from. He said Rocky Mount and it went on from there. We were neighboring cities. We talked about landmarks and what we did when we went to each other cities. He said he was the first-shift baker and if I wanted anything to let him know and he would take care of it for me.

After I finished shaping him up, we talked a little more and then he gave me soup and a bag of chips. I wasn't expecting anything because I was thinking I was still under review, so to speak. The next four that I cut were pretty cool as well. Some left stamps, others left food.

Reid and I talked as we waited for the next two to make their way down. He said that he went to a barber school called Black World in Charlotte, NC. I had never heard of that one before and he had never heard of Harris Barber School. He said that we were just about done for the day and that he was surprised that we had knocked out the whole dorm so early. Three guys came in then at the same time.

One went directly to Reid's chair, one sat in the waiting chair, and the other one sat in my chair. The whole vibe shifted. I knew something was up. The guy that sat in my chair was a lanky, red-complexioned guy. Violence and pain were etched in his face. His eyes penetrated your entire being, as if searching for that weak spot to take advantage of. You could tell he visited the weight-pile quite regular. I put my drape on him and asked him what kind of cut he wanted.

He turned around, looked up at me, and said, "I want a bald fade. I ain't got shit for you, and if you fuck my head up, I'm gone fuck you up."

I laughed it off and made sure I had the right length on top, because I knew he had every intention on trying to fight if the cut wasn't up to his standards. During the blending process his neck got stiff, which wouldn't allow me to turn his head to get a good look at my work.

He wasn't saying anything so, I said, "Damn if you going to keep a stiff neck, I can't cut your hair right. Loosen up."

Reid and his client chuckled a little bit, but this guy held a stone face. The guy sitting in the waiting chair was torn between smiling and not, so he just bit his lip. The guy in my chair loosened up a little bit. I could tell he didn't like to take orders, yet his very existence thrived on him giving orders.

Once I finished, I handed him the mirror. He got out of the chair and inspected every angle of the cut. After he finished looking, he sat back down and said, "Get the back of my neck and you good."

I tightened the drape and got the hair on his neck, put some astringent on him, and he stuck his hand out for a pound. I touched his fist with mine and then he and the other guy walked out together. The tension left the air.

I asked Reid what was that all about. He said that's L.A and Grape. They were some Crips from California that ran a lot of the Crips on the yard. "The next time you cut his hair, he will talk. Grape is a cool dude. He just mean as hell. The other guy that came in with him was his trigger man. He stays with him wherever he goes."

After that encounter, I wanted a cigarette. I went to the yard and took a quick smoke. I was glad I didn't get fly out of the mouth. One reason I wasn't upset was because I understood the intimidation tactics of some of the older, more seasoned penitentiary vets.

A haircut was like an exclusive thing because you could get only one per month, and that doesn't include the face. To have the barber on the team was a major thing. I had been expecting to run across more attempts at intimidation, and other approaches of winning me over, and having me in their corner.

After our day had come to an end, Reid and I went outside to smoke. I pulled out a Newport and offered one to him. He declined. He didn't smoke shorts. He said that he wanted the whole damn cigarette, not a sample, and they were like inhaling air. I thought that was pretty funny and watched him pull out some Newport longs.

"Damn heart buster," I said. "Them shits remind me of a damn Kool."

He laughed and said that's why he smoked them because that's what he smoked in the streets. I found it quite hilarious how we had a preference on the way we soothed our anxieties, which slowly worked against our physical health.

The barbershop quickly became my little hangout. Even when I had no clients, I would find myself working on my tools and listening to music. More listening than working, but that was my excuse to get my clipper box and go to the shop. Some officers would come and check on me from time to time to see what I was hiding or putting together. Some would be frank and ask me outright. I told them I was putting together my

105

mind and hiding nothing. Other officers would welcome the idea of me going in and chilling. As long as I wasn't bothering anyone, I was good. Reid told me that he stayed out there as much as he could. He had been the barber on the unit for about three years and was burned out.

One Monday, I was cleaning my clippers and an officer called me to the booth to report to my case manager's office. I had no idea what to expect. I was good with my barber job. I hadn't done anything wrong to my knowledge. When I reached Ms. Perry's office, she was standing behind her desk. She looked up when she heard my knock and waved for me to come.

She told me to follow her to the conference room. She said I wasn't supposed to come until 10:30, so I was like twenty minutes early. In the conference room I found a single chair facing the two long tables. There were two other case managers already seated, discussing their daily agendas. I was confused when I saw the setup. I was asked to have a seat and told the reason for my being there. It was my custody review.

They were actually considering me for medium custody. I got knots in my stomach and all of a sudden, I got gas. They asked me all types of questions, like how did I feel about sleeping in an open dorm with 30 to 40 others. They asked about my mental state, working on the road squad, a lot of questions were self-explanatory if they had read my chart. But it was cool going through the formalities. They conversed among themselves, told me that I could possibly hear a response within the month, and then I was dismissed.

When I got back to the block everyone knew I had just left my custody review. They asked me all types of questions. Where was I going? What type of questions did they ask you? Some people congratulated me. I got my door popped while answering their questions and smoked a cigarette, trying to take the whole thing in. I had gotten a little comfortable where I was and honestly wasn't too sure if I was happy about the possibility of being moved. I wasn't even sure if I was going to get my medium. Dre and CLIP had gotten their medium custody and left two weeks prior to me having my review. I had no idea where they went, but I had an idea where I wanted to go if I made it. Johnson County and Franklin County were my top two choices, since they was close to Wilson.

I wanted a tattoo bad. I really didn't know what I wanted, so I looked at tattoo and hip-hop magazines to get some ideas. I wanted to honor my grandmother who had recently passed, so I decided to get an angel with her name inscribed above it and her years of birth and death. I didn't have far to go to find an artist because we had one of the best right in the block with us.

He was a cool, older, white guy with a bald head that went by the name Fruit Loop. Fruit Loop was known to get high on pills and smoke weed on the regular. I never heard anything bad about his work, so I decided to give him a shot. He said that he respected his craft enough not to get high on pills and do any work. I showed him what I wanted and he charged me $10. I felt like that was a reasonable price, so I paid him half upfront. He wanted to draw it up and make sure that I approved of the rough drafts. Once he got it together, I checked it out and approved of everything. We were going to proceed with it the next day. I wanted to get it done Sunday through Tuesday so it wouldn't be fresh when I went to visitation. I made a mental note of everything that he wanted and got guys to get that item when they asked me what I wanted when I cut their hair.

Once it was time to get it done, I almost chumped out, but my money was already paid and I couldn't use anything that I'd given him. I went back on my word and smoked a joint and damn near a half a pack of Newports. The process wasn't bad at all. It had been such a long while since I'd last gotten one that I forgot the pain level. Once the needle stopped I was numb to the pain. I took a look at it and my cheeks touched my eyes. I was so happy that I had the privilege of carrying my grandmother's name with me for the entirety of my existence.

Two weeks went by and I noticed that my grandmother's name wasn't spelled right. I was a little hurt and upset for a while so, I figured I'd wait a while and gather my thoughts on the proper way to address the situation. I knew it was an honest mistake obviously. I didn't want to put emotions in the mix and say the wrong thing to cause a problem.

When I was coming in the block from work, I saw Fruit Loop coming in from the canteen. I pulled him to the side and told him the situation, went into his room, and rolled my thermal sleeve up so I could show it to him. His reaction matched mine. I totally respected this type of conversation.

He looked at the entire tattoo and said, "Hell, I'll do the whole damn thing over for you in about two weeks because it's a little light too."

I walked out happy with my coolness, and the way that I handled the situation. I went to my room and smoked a cigarette and read about Deadwood Dick, a black cowboy in a book that I found in my room.

I went to the shop just to kick it with my man, Reid. He always had something slick to put me up on, whether it was game or just something that he had experienced during his bid. I always appreciated it when an older guy shared his insight.

One day we were in the shop, just kicking it about nothing in particular but everything and a guy from the warehouse came in. He said that the Christmas packages had just arrived and we would be getting them once the third shift got in. Shit. I was excited because I had a little something on the way. I knew that I had a lot of stuff that I needed to clean up in my room, so that was my task for the day. Reid and I looked at our daily list of cuts and we didn't have anymore. We cleaned up the shop and our clippers, turned in our clippers, and went to the dorm.

While I was cleaning my room, Wise came by and asked me if I was shipping out. I laughed because I knew I was up for my medium custody but hadn't heard any results as of yet.

"Nah, man. The Christmas packages are here and I'm just trying to make some room for all this shit."

We talked about the Moorish Science Temple and how he was trying to build it back up from the dismantling that the administration had done earlier in the year. He was kind of stressed about that. It was kind of his subtle way of asking me to take on a role in the temple. I told him that I was studying the Rastafarian culture at the time, however, and that if I wasn't, I would definitely take a position. I wanted to stay true to me and not mix too much up right then. We smoked a cigarette, and then he said was going to his room to do the same. He closed the door and walked off, looking a little dejected. I chilled in my room, wrote, and listened to music until they called our dorm for Christmas packages.

They called individuals down by dorm and blocks, so it was a slight pandemonium with everyone wanting to be at the front of the line in their block. A couple of shoving matches took place in each block's line. Even people who weren't getting anything were excited. They knew that they would get something from someone in a generous and giving mood.

Just like other Christmases, while in line I planned on looking out for those who weren't getting anything. This had become my yearly ritual for a while and I couldn't let it go. I saw it as my yearly tithe, and I looked forward to doing it. I knew it could be taken as a sign of weakness on the adult spread, but I had already committed to it my first two years. I wasn't at all caught up in the holiday thing, but if I had some extra to give, I would share with someone. It didn't necessarily have to be someone I dealt with, just someone I thought had a good character. I would fix a small bag for them. Although I didn't eat meat, I would order a couple of meat items just to lookout for others.

I finally made it to the hall where they were giving out boxes. The officer asked me my name and opus number. I told him and they had a problem finding my box. I was asked to step to the side while they looked for mine and retrieved other people's boxes. I knew that I had a box. My family told me they had ordered it for me. The officer called me to give it to me when they found it. He said they had it in another pile and asked me if I made my medium custody. I gave him a puzzled look. Why did it matter and how did he of all people know that I had a custody review?

"Nah, not that I know of."

I transferred the contents of the box into the bag that was issued with the box and went back to my block. Once I got back to my room, I turned on my radio and put the earbuds at the bottom of the two holes of my Styrofoam cup to create a surround sound system. I dumped the contents of my box on the bed and properly organized everything. I needed to get to sleep, so I decided I would make the bags for the next day.

The next day I followed my daily routine: work, yard, chow, and writing a letter or two. I observed to see who didn't get anything. I figured I could fix at least two bags and still be straight. I'd made sure that all my homeboys were good from Wilson first and then I'd seek out others. I would slide the two bags to whoever my heart lead me to give them to, but it slipped my mind again. Once we were locked down for the night, I decided to get it done since I had a little energy.

I made a little mat on the floor with my extra blanket and began to sort through everything that I was willing to part with. Just as I began, I heard my door pop. That was one of the last things you wanted to hear without hearing the sliders opening first. I folded the blanket up so I could get some grip on the floor if there was going to be a tussle. I heard the slider door open and an officer came to my door. He asked me how many bags I needed.

My heart dropped because I had no clue that I'd made medium custody. I said I'd take the max. I didn't have many personal items other than books; however, I did have a lot from the Christmas package. He returned with four bags and said that he was sorry, but I had to make it all fit. I was cool with that because I knew I could and, you best believe it, I did. He said that someone would be coming through to get me around five o'clock. He shook my hand and commended me on my progress. I went from packing to give something away to packing to go away.

I packed my things in a hurry and tried my best to get some rest because wake-up was not far off. I smoked a cigarette while I packed, and once I was finished I tried to find sleep. Another officer came by later and popped my lock. He told me they were ready for me.

I was escorted to the chow hall where I met the other guys who were shipping out. We made small talk and ate all that we were given. We were then ushered into the holding cell where we waited on the transfer bus to arrive. We continued our small talk until we grew tired of sitting. Some of them became sleepy, others grew restless. I was filled with a mix of emotions, nervousness, excitement, and everything else. This would be my first ride on the "state goose." I wanted to get the ball rolling. It was cold and I was growing impatient.

Around six-thirty, the bus pulls up. I didn't know the ropes, so I fell back and watched others get on and then mimicked them. They gave their bags to one officer and got on the back of the bus. I climbed in and found an empty seat in the middle. Although it was my first time riding, I knew not to sit in the back with the "john/jacket," also known as the toilet.

They were taking us to Sandy Ridge. I could finally see what Petty Pablo was talking about in his hit song *North Carolina*. We stopped at five other prisons along the way, picking up guys in browns and greens. Although I had almost a decade to go, I still fantasized about getting my greens. That's how I cut my riding time, between that and looking out the window, fantasizing about going home.

When we reached Sandy Ridge, it looked like some kind of slave encampment. There were two buildings and each had two pens. The pens held all of the transferring inmates. In one building, they wear brown clothes and in the other building, they wear green clothes. I still saw a sprinkle of each in the mix with each other. I saw guys I hadn't seen in a couple of years from the streets and Polk. I kicked it with the guys until names were called for us to get on our respective buses. We listened carefully, waiting to see which bus would take us to our plantation. When my name was called, I dapped up the fellows, and wished them luck on their journeys. As I got on the bus, I was asked my name and opus number and then told me to have a seat.

As I nestled into my seat, my thoughts ran wild. I no longer fantasized about having greens or being home. I began

114

to wrap my mind around starting a new mission in a new place. I focused on the mantra: The journey continues. Where one road stops, another takes its place.

Chapter 4

BLINDLY SEEKING

After leaving Polk and Pasquotank, I didn't feel there were too many places they could put me that would intimidate me. After that long bus ride from one side of the state to almost the other end, and the long stop at Sandy Ridge, by the time I reached my destination I was dog tired. I had no intention of trying to find any homeboys or meet anyone. I just wanted to get some rest.

I quickly made my bunk, put up my personal belongings, and attempted to call home, but I was denied because I didn't have a PIN number. I called a guy over to assist me with my call. He seemed pretty cool and let me use his pin until I was assigned one. I just wanted to let my family know where I had been relocated.

No sooner than my mother pressed 5 on the keypad to accept my call, an officer peeped his head through the sliding door and said, "Ronald Bullock you are needed in the library."

The officer let the door slide shut, so I finished briefing my mother. When I told her where I was, which was actually across the state from her, I could tell she was upset, by her tone After our call, I walked to the door and my mind wandered all the way back to Wilson, to my mother's couch, as if I could console her. The doors reopened and the officer motioned for me to come with her. She led me to the library with the two other guys who transferred in with me. When we entered we were instructed to sit in front of a stack of paper at the table. The paper was a sign off on our PIN numbers for the phone. We were told to not allow anyone to use it and to not use anyone else's or we would get a write-up. Great, I'd already broken one rule without even knowing.

I was finally able to get a little rest. I had grown accustomed to a single cell, so I would have to adjust to sleeping in an open dorm again. I tossed and turned the entire night. Once I settled in, the lights came on and the doors opened. Two officers came in and yelled count time. The count times that I'd grown used to were officers looking into your room and counting you while you were doing whatever you wanted to do. This count time was totally different. It woke me from my nap and required me to stand beside my bunk until the count was completed for the block. The process was just plain hateful. It was just another demeaning mental tactic on another plantation. Every plantation has its way of reminding you of your status. No matter how much peace you seek, they have a way of bringing you back to your harsh reality.

I knew the camp was close to Charlotte so I expected to see a few guys from the area who I knew from Polk. I made it to breakfast and ran into two guys I knew, C-Slim and Rham. We ate together and they introduced me to some of their people. They made sure I was good with the guys in the clothes house and got some new clothes.

C-Slim was waiting on the feds to come get him and Rham was on his way home. When C-Slim found out that we were in the same unit, he asked me if I still cut hair. He said the unit's barber just went to the hole for fighting so the position was open. BINGO! That was it. I had a mission.

I told him I would talk to my case manager and put in that request. He asked if I know Dank from Wilson. "Shit. All you gotta do is holla at him and he can get your foot in the door, 'cause your case manager is not going to call you for a while."

Finding Dank turned out to be my mission for the moment. Rham, always the jokester, said, "You know that you can't be overcharging these dudes for that whack ass fade!"

We all laughed, emptied our trays, and dapped each other up. I kicked it with the guy from the clothes house and gave him my sizes, so he would have me some clothes set to the side. As they hung back and talked, I walked to the dorm with my thoughts racing, but found myself chuckling about what Rham had said. When I get to my block, I see that there are two chairs at the end of the bunk, not only mine but for the most part, all of them. For some reason I hadn't noticed this last night. I guess fatigue and being irritable was one reason.

I saw my bunkie making his bunk so I introduced myself. He was an older white guy with white hair. I extended my hand and could sense his hesitancy. That made it more enjoyable when he finally grabbed my hand.

I gave him a nice firm grip and said, "Nice to meet you just hate the current situation."

He gave me what looked like a fabricated smile and said his name was J.T. Since I had his attention, I asked him about the chairs.

"Look on the back and you'll see that each chair has a bunk number on it. While I'm at it, don't sit on my bunk, and if you can help it, when you get off yours, don't step on mine!"

I felt the vibe from the introduction, but this was his exclamation mark. If I hadn't learned anything else thus far, I'd definitely learned to respect people's space.

It had just rained so the yard was not going to open. That meant I wouldn't get a chance to see Dank unless I met him in the chow hall. Since I didn't know anyone in my block, I took my chair from the bunk area and into the dayroom so I could watch the TV since I didn't feel like talking to anyone in particular at the time. Nothing but music videos were on, so I decided to read the newspaper. We didn't get *The News & Observer* that I'd grown accustomed to, but we did get *The Charlotte Observer.*

The Charlotte Observer was like reading French. I recognized the characters, but could not put them together, I was in a new region. As I looked at the paper, the guy who had let me use his PIN number asked if he could get the front page once I finished.

"Bet," I said.

He asked me where I had come from, where I was from, and what made me pick this camp out of all camps. I found out this was always the icebreaker—the real feel-you-out-type questions. I told him I came from Pasquotank, I was from Wilson, and I came there because I didn't have any say in the matter since I had just made my medium custody. Pasquotank needed space so "here" was my destination.

I extended my hand and introduced myself. I got the usual response—the question mark face and "say that one more time." I'm always ready to repeat myself when I say my name, so I said, "Udy," once again.

He watched my mouth and said it with me. He said it a couple more times and then, "Udy, I'm Dread." We forgot all about the paper then. "You did say that you are from Wilson, right? I think Dank is from Wilson," he added.

"Yeah. My man C-Slim was telling me about him!" I said.

"You know C-Slim too? Shit. You straight. You really don't need to know nobody else!"

Damn what had I run up on? He told me what was going on, on the yard, and who was who. He saw that my little locks were beginning to sprout, so he asked me a question only a person "striving" on the path would ask.

"Are your locks fashion or are they the Lion's Mane?"

My mouth could not utter the words fast enough, because I was happy to have run across an "Elder"—a true Lion's Mane Elder! He smiled and we both stood in unison

, shook hands and embraced. We kicked it for a while and he told me he wanted to take me to meet the other brothers. We made our rounds through the next pods. I hadn't known they existed until then. When we reached the adjoining block, we spotted the other "Breddren" on the top tier, sitting at the table, talking and laughing.

"Breddren, this is Udy. He's a Young Lion!"

"Wha' gwan idren. Where de I dem from," asked a light-skinned Breddern with a small crown on.

"I'm from Wilson."

"Oh Jah, you know de Breddren Dank?"

"I gotta see him," I said. "What's his real name?"

"Peace and blessings. I'm K.K Do you know Shell Dell?"

"Hell, yeah that my dude, he left me at Polk!"

"That's one hustling ass dude, good dude!" K.K said.

We all talked, and when chow was called, we all went together and waited for them to call the dorm that Dank slept in. As we went through the line, I saw that they were serving chicken and the regular cheese sandwich for the sub, so I got the chicken and gave it to the Breddren to split and just ate my sides. A little later, I saw C-Slim walk through the door. I get up to meet him and we dapped each other up. He said he thought Dank was on the way. Waiting to meet Dank almost began to feel like going to the park when you were a kid. It was like a big deal.

I was kind of expecting to see a big, tall, loud guy with locks or something. When he walked in, they pointed out a short, dark-skinned brother who looked familiar, I just couldn't place him. After he finally went through the line to get his tray, he came and sat at the table with Kaya, K.K, and myself. The Elder Dread had just left, leaving a seat open for Dank to sit.

I introduced myself, told him what side of town I was from, and who my people were. We began to go back and forth about who we knew, and not much to my surprise, we knew a lot of the same people. Not like Wilson was that big, I'm just shocked that we never crossed paths before. After we finished eating, we sat and talked until the chow hall closed, and then we all walked to our respective dorms. It was late December, so it was dark by the time we left. Kaya, K.K, and I reached our dorm first. We all smoked a cigarette and watched as Dank faded into the dusk.

The next day the yard finally opened so I got a chance to go out and check it out. This yard was the farthest thing from what I'd grown to know as a yard over the past couple years. It only consisted of a half-court for basketball, a horseshoe pit, a small weight pile, a couple of benches, and just enough room to walk a small lap. They said that the big yard was supposed to offset this small miniature yard we were confined to on a daily basis, yet very seldom did we see the big yard. Anyway, since I got up early and the yard was open, I went out to get me an early smoke and to get a feel for everything. As I smoked my Newport, I leaned on the wall and did some people watching. I looked at who interacted with who and who spoke with whom. I witnessed early morning plays being made. I wasn't a chain smoker by a long shot, yet I didn't want to go back into the dorm to watch the TV. I definitely didn't want to deal with my bunkmate's shenanigans this early, so I half-smoked the next cigarette. Just as I was getting tired of the toxic fumes, Dank stepped out of his dorm.

I've always been kind of apprehensive about being too lively with others in the morning because everyone isn't a morning person. It takes some longer than others to adjust; however, I asked him if he wanted the rest of the cigarette before I threw it out. He took it and that seemed to be somewhat of our icebreaker. Once again we talked about Wilson and who we knew and who we've run across on state and what they had going on. I told him I was cutting hair at Pasquotank before I was shipped out. He asked me if I wanted to cut hair on the unit, and I assured him that I did.

He told me that the barber job was open, so he could talk to some people to see if I could get in the barbershop. That was cool because I was kind of freelancing my sentence at that point. This would give me a little structure for the time being. I asked him why everyone gave him so much praise around the yard. He said he wasn't sure, he was just him, and he showed everyone respect. That I was sure of; however, I was damn well sure it was more than just being a guy of integrity, but I dared not pry.

Later that day, I was sitting at a table playing chess with a guy just to pass time, something I found myself doing more than usual lately. I hear my name being called in the adjoining block, so I went to see what I was needed for. The redhead lady officer told me I was needed in the case manager's office down the hall. When I stepped in, I noticed a nice-looking, older, black lady. You could tell she had taken care of herself because she had aged gracefully. I recalled my first encounter with Ms. Perry and waited to be asked before I took a seat. She said I was one of the first to do that, and thanked me. I was shocked at her politeness because I heard that she could be impolite and that was putting what I'd heard mildly.

She said the unit had a barber job open at the time and she saw that I had quite a few hours of working in the barbershop since I'd been on state. She was basically offering me the job. I kindly accepted, and she then pulled out papers for me to sign. After that she sent me to the sergeant's office to have them give me the rules and get me logged into the system as the unit's barber. When I met the sergeant, I wasn't sure who peed in his cereal that day, but he brought it with him to work. He said this was his unit and no one was supposed to give the barber job away until they consulted him first. He called the other barber to the office and introduced us so we could come up with our weekly schedule.

The other barber was a white guy who was attempting to pass as a Native American. I already knew that he had an issue being himself, so I knew that he couldn't be real with me. During the meeting with him and the sergeant, I was a little confused as to who was the government official and who was the inmate. The barber had as many rules as the sergeant. I disregarded both of them because I knew right from wrong. They told me that I would start work the very next day. I was excited and nervous at the same time. The barber told me it would work better if I worked the second shift since there weren't as many straight-haired people. The older white guys stayed in the dorms while the majority of the coarse-hair guys went to school during the day. I was cool with that, I was just happy to have the clippers back in my hand.

My first day on the job fell on a Friday. There wasn't any school because they were out for Christmas break, so I was sure that no matter how skeptical they were they had to come in and give me a try because everyone wanted to be fresh for visitation. The very first thing I did was set my blades according to my personal preference. I found a good radio station because I could not cut with the bluegrass that the other barber had playing. Just as I found Power 98, my first client walked through the door.

He was an older guy, maybe in his late forties or early fifties, and very mild-mannered. He said, "How long have you been cutting youngin?"

"Since I was in middle school," I responded.

"Well, I just want a butt naked fade. Just take a little off the top. Now you know everyone wants to see what you are working with, so you gotta do me right!"

The latter part of his statement I knew was true and he was exactly right. I did have to put him in the game. I already knew my plight was to be as he stated it, so I took the rhythm of the music and allowed my body to sync with it.

During the course of his haircut, people would casually walk by the door and look in, while others were not as subtle. Once I finished him, I handed him the mirror. He stood up and bounced mirror off mirror reflection to check the entirety of the cut and sat back down. His facial expression and body language told me what I needed to know.

"Good job youngin!" He left and returned with a couple of chips and cakes. "I gotta take care of the barber," he stated in a matter-of-fact way.

The next person who came in, introduced himself as Country Mike. As he sat down, he asked, "Can you do a temp?"

He had an aggressive personality, which is a tactic I've grown accustomed to. Some guys think they can intimidate a good haircut out of the barber. When he sat down, I allowed him to do all the talking. He told me about all the close custody camps that he has been on and his attempt to run his penitentiary intimidation game. He talked with his hands and used body gestures. I turned my clippers off, looked at him, and listened. He stopped talking and looked at me as if I committed an error.

"Mike, there is no way I can give you a good haircut if you can't sit still!"

I said it to show him I wasn't affected by his act. He got the picture and toned down his act. After we cleared the air, we began to dialogue.

He told me that he had been locked up since he was eighteen. He was thirty-four and had four more years until his release date. Once we began to talk civil, his haircut was over.

"Yo, you laced me, boy. Do you smoke?"

"I do."

"Take these ten Newports, and I'll see you next week. While you are bullshitting, you need to put up a piece of paper on the door and start you a list, 'cause you going to get packed when they see what you can do."

I took his advice and went to the officer's desk and got a piece of paper and some tape. I took the pencil from my cabinet drawer and tied dental floss around it and hung the paper and pencil up outside of the door. Slowly, I noticed people signing up and peeping in the door to inquire about getting a fresh visitation cut. When I left for the day, I accumulated a big bag of canteen, all assorted snacks. I knew the sergeant would be looking for me to make an erroneous move, so I got K.K to come by and pick up my earnings periodically. He was paid as well for his services. Dank used to do the same before he shipped out.

The next morning Kaya and Dread came by to wake me for the Rastafarian service. I was excited because this would be my very first Rastafarian service ever. Kaya and K.K had their hands full of books and folders, so I jubilantly assisted with the load. The hunger and eagerness to arrive at the destination and learn showed in my face. As we arrived, we moved chairs and tables to fit our preference. Once we hung the Lion of Judah flag, we set the vibe with the Killamanjaro mixtape, and then set up the True-brary (library). Once the vibes were set, Kaya would take the podium and begin to teach us about the culture, and then we would reason (discuss) the topic of that day. Just to hear the tunes (reggae music) was therapeutic, and enough to set a positive vibe for the next week. This would be my Saturday ritual for as long as I had control of my being.

I've never been too big on the celebration of any holidays other than birthdays because that's the only thing that I myself could prove. So when Christmas came around, I wasn't too thrilled with nor did I participate in any of the camp festivities. I was just ready for it to pass so that the New Year could come and the system could get back on its regular schedule. When the system slowed, mail stopped. When mail stopped, it seemed as if time stood still. I found these times to be the most depressing because mail was my main source of contact with the world.

One day, I slid off to the barbershop and made it my haven for clearing my mind. I sat and listened to slow jams, a little of Sade, O'Jays, Anita Baker, and Prince. Countless others came across the radio as I sat and allowed my thoughts to take me to the comfort of my room at my parents' house. While I lost myself in my thoughts, I heard a knock on the door. It was the redheaded female officer and she abruptly snapped me back to prison.

"It's count time and you need to stay in here until it clears!"

When count cleared I linked up with Kaya, K.K, and Dread, and I put together some soups, beans, and rice, and fish. Kaya cooked each of us a bowl. Mine was just beans, rice, and noodles. During our festivities, we talked, and I noticed that each of them had multiple diplomas in different trades. This was interesting because they all seemed to like going to school and could give you a breakdown of the course that they were in at that point.

I had taken a couple of certificate classes at Polk, but to get a diploma was another level. To go to school sounded a little intimidating to me. I guess it was written on my face of how shocked I was, so they assured me that if I really wanted to, I could definitely do it. Somewhere in the midst of the conversation, one of them brought out a speech by H.I.M Haile Selassie I.

It was on education and its importance. I read it and since that day it was one of my personal favorite speeches by H.I.M. From that point, I vowed that I would chase an education for the remainder of my sentence. I could not stop thinking about making my parents proud of me by turning my prison sentence into an informal college stay. I began to talk to all of my clients about higher education and how I longed for it. Of course, I was smart enough to know who to hold that conversation with. I was trying to pick individuals' brains on the road to take to attain this sudden dream of an education.

It's amazing how you can will things in your direction by the vibration of words. I've heard that the universe hears you when you speak. I was about to close the shop up one day just to shoot ball while everyone was in school. As I started cleaning my clippers, a guy walked through the door and asked if I could give him a cut. He introduced himself as William, but he went by Will.

I've seen him around, but this was our first time formally meeting each other. He said the other barber usually cut his hair because he didn't like the barber that had the job prior to me. He said he had seen my work and wanted to give me a shot. Will didn't have a difficult haircut at all. He got an even all over with a taper in the back, not difficult at all for any somewhat-skilled barber.

I started to go into my higher education spiel, and he told me that he was a college graduate. He said it was pleasing to hear a young black man talk about education. He asked what I wanted to take up. In spite of all the talk about wanting an education, I really couldn't answer that question. I thought about it and said I wanted to take a business class and some computer courses.

Will said he knew someone in the system that knew someone else who could make the necessary moves for me, if I wrote to the right people. He coached me through the entire writing process. Once we hit all of the proper targets, it became a waiting game.

Will could not tell me what he didn't know, but one day while cutting his hair he told me that within the next month or so I should hear something. My anxiety grew, and uncertainty began to grow. I signed up for a certificate computer class just in case the transfer falls through. K.K told me if I really wanted to know if I was going to ship out, I should make sure that I have a library book checked out.

When you have a library book checked out in your name, the library man would find you throughout the course of the day. If you tried to check a book out, he wouldn't let you because you would be removed from the population system.

After I learned that, I would go to the library every Monday and Wednesday because the shipping day was Tuesday and Thursday.

One day in June of 2003, I went to the library and the librarian would not allow me to check out a book. His excuse was that the computer was showing that I had a book out, a book that I had turned in earlier. I hadn't even read it. It was just part of my weekly plot to see if I was shipping.

I said I would go and see if I could find the book and come back tomorrow to turn it in. I could hardly fight the smile and elation in my spirit as I spoke. I quickly hit the yard in search of Will after I sent word for him to come out. He emerged from behind the door with a big grin on his face as if he got the word at the same time I did. I thanked him and promised him that I would do my best and take every class that I possibly could. And most of all, I would get my degree in business. He let me know that I would run across a lot of distractions but to stay focused and keep my word. He also said that once he finished a couple of classes at Albemarle, he would be on his way to Harnett also. I thanked him again and then we went to our dorms.

My mind was racing. I didn't know where to start because I didn't want to show that I knew that I was shipping. That would show them there was a flaw in their system, which could cause them to change their way of doing things. I didn't want that at all, so I calmed down and went to kick it with Kaya, K.K, and Dread. I thanked them for opening my eyes to this education thing. I knew that I didn't like school when I was forced to go, but this was an entirely different scenario. I was actually volunteering to go to school.

Kaya made me promise that if the camp didn't have a Rastafarian service that I would establish one. I reluctantly agreed. I didn't know the proper channels to start, but I knew it was possible. As long as there was a will, there was a way.

He gave me a folder full of papers and assured me that this would be beneficial in my endeavors to get the job done.

I linked up with the Breddren after that. We went to dinner and just vibed with each other and reasoned. We exchanged information with intentions of linking up or at least staying in contact with each other. Later that night, when the phones were cut off and all daily activities had ceased, I was called to the sergeant's office and told that I would be shipping to Harnett in the morning. He asked me how many shipping bags I needed. At this point, I haven't accumulated much so I only needed three bags. The feeling was surreal. I had literally talked my way into this situation. I was on my way to pursue a vague dream. I was totally elated, nervous, excited, and confused. The mix of emotions was never-ending. All in all, I just gave thanks and praise to the Most High for the opportunity to move forward in a positive manner.

As usual, the officer woke me in the wee hours of the morning to prepare for my long day of Sandy Ridge and a bus ride that I definitely wasn't looking forward to.

Chapter 5

LEARNING TO LEARN

Finally reaching my desired camp, I've arrived at college. All praises due to The Most High. I was sent to Harnett Correctional Center, the place filled with dreams and hopes—a place of betterment. Upon my arrival, I had my mind set on growth and preparing myself for my exodus into the free world. With this being my task, I decided to put my childishness behind me and create a circle with those who saw life from a perspective that was foreign to me. Guys who I would once considered lame became my intended acquaintance. Harnett Correctional had a population of a thousand inmates, so there should be a lot individuals for me to seek out. With an associate and bachelor degree programs in Business Administration and diploma programs in carpentry, welding, masonry, electrical wiring, and electrical service technology, among other certificate classes, there was enough education to occupy the remaining nine years of my sentence.

During in-processing, we went through the normal routine: strip search, property search, issued a new set of browns and change of clothes, and get assigned our housing location. After that our journey as a resident of the facility could begin.

When I finished gathering my belongings from the processing officer, he informed me that Harnett was a cash facility. We didn't need to use our ID card at the canteen. I hadn't seen or held any cash in years. So the officer asked me how much money I wanted. I took twenty dollars to be on the safe side. My wheels began to turn. Thousand inmates and cash. The math was great. I wasn't the fastest guy, but by far was I wasn't the slowest. The path to education and changing my life would be one hell of a test.

Walking through the big ass camp, I got lost and ran into a homeboy named Paz. I knew him from the streets of my hometown. A known dope boy in the streets, I knew he would have something popping on a cash camp. We went through the where did you come from, how long you been down routine. I asked him to point me in the right direction to my dorm, so I could put the heavy ass mattress cover down. It was filled with all of my personal belongings. I told him we'd link up once I made up my bed and put my things in my locker. While I was unpacking, lil Tee and Green Eye, two guys who I knew from Polk came through to check me out.

"Man, hurry up and get your shit together so we can go blow one," lil Tee said. Just that quick I was being tested. I didn't want to walk around this new camp, not on point, so I told lil Tee I was good. The last thing I wanted was to get caught off guard and not able to properly defend myself.

After I put all my things in my locker and made my bunk, I linked up with lil Tee. He gave me a tour of the yard and took me around to see the rest of the people I knew from Polk. While walking, I noticed he was doing his gang handshake, one of the kind of things I was still staying away from. Believe it or not, the universe has a way of testing you to see if you are as sincere as you profess to be.

On our search for these dudes, we ran into a lot of guys I knew from the youth spread, and other camps, but I was really trying to link back up with Paz. I wanted to see what was really going on as well as who he was kicking it with in the streets. I eventually broke away from lil Tee and the rest of the youth spread crew. I needed to walk alone, see what was popping, and what energy my locks would attract.

On my solo journey, I walked down the shoot (the walkway in the middle of the camp which lead to all the dormitories). It seemed like the shoot was at least half a mile long. On my quest to see the ins and outs of the camp, I was rolled up on by two big country dudes. I had no clue who they were or how they knew me, but I was definitely glad I hadn't smoked now for real.

"Your name Udy," asked the one with the glasses.

"We heard you are from Wilson," said the other one who still had workout gloves on.

I guess they saw in my eyes that they'd put me on the defense, so I replied, "Yeah. I'm from Wilson. What's good?"

They looked at each other and busted out laughing as if they knew something I didn't.

"Man, you cool. We from Wide-A-Wake too. I'm Boston and this is Big Stan."

The lump in my throat loosened up. I was happy as hell to have these two muscle-bound dudes on the team. We walked and talked and linked up with Paz and another homeboy named Eric. They all gave me the rundown on who was who and what was what. I found out that all the homeboys had their hand in something. From loaning money, card games, running numbers, canteens, cigarettes, and on down to bookies, the list was long. It was great feeling like I was in the right spot with the right team. With that solidified, I could focus on my major mission.

After chow I went to my dorm to take a nap. The lady C.O. told me to pack my things because I was moving to another dorm because this was the kitchen dorm. After three days on the camp and I was already moving. I was just ready to settle in and begin some type of routine so I could add some structure to my bid.

My next move was up the hill to "A" dorm. This was a dorm with people who worked, went to school, and just bidding. It would give me the chance to really see from other people what was going on around the camp rather than just my homeboys' perspectives. Not that there was anything wrong with theirs. I just wanted to broaden my horizons. That had been my reason for transferring to Harnett.

On my first night in A-dorm, I went into the dayroom and sat at the table with my bag of popcorn and water and people-watched as the people watched TV. I was determined to learn. I was aware of the fact that education was the key to a better future. I wanted it, formal and informal alike. What would I do with it once I'd attained it?

On day two in A-dorm, I was approached by a short guy, named "Ra-Born," from Raleigh, as we prepared to go to lunch.

"What's up, young buck. I see you are observant."

I didn't know how to respond, so I said, "Yeah. I like to see what I'm in the midst of."

"That's what you are supposed to do. You a little sharp too, huh?"

We walked to the chow hall together. We talked about Polk, getting locked up as teenagers, and catching over a decade in the penitentiary. With an attribute such as Rah-Born, I assumed he was a member of the 5 percenter Nation, of which I was a truant student. As we sat at the chow table and so randomly said, "Peace God I be the God Valuable-Jewel, God Allah!"

He looked at me and said, "Leave that shit on the youth spread!" and chuckled.

I was totally dumbfounded. I was sure his name was a divine attribute of Allah. I knew from observation guys from Raleigh were a little more on the cultural side of things. He went on to explain that he use to study the "lessons," but he fell away from them because they weren't helping him in the direction he was going. I guess I could understand that.

I found Rah-Born to be an interesting character. He told me he had gotten his associate's degree in business when he was at "Foot Hills," which was a youth institution. He was now getting his bachelor's through the Shaw program offered at the camp, another piece to the puzzle. I told him my desire to do the same, and from that point on I depicted him as one of my silent mentors.

Walking aimlessly just trying to figure out my way around that huge camp, I decided to go to the gym. On my way there, I heard, "Yo, home-team." It came from a loud, deep voice yelling down the shoot. The same voice called out twice more and then yelled my name.

I looked through the crowd of faces, and a sea of brown clothes. Then I saw the familiar face jumping up and down with his hand waving hand-waving.

"What's good Paz?" I asked, walking toward him.

He stopped a couple of times to exchange roll-ups (Top's self-rolled cigarettes) for money. We finally linked up and headed toward the bottom of the shoot to find some more homeboys. When we reached the bottom, I witnessed penitentiary hustle in its purest form. It was like I was back in the hood. Everything you wanted, needed, and didn't need, you could find at the bottom. Porn books, Walkmans, headphones, any type of drug, visitation clothes, shoes, food from the chow hall. Shit, you could buy and borrow money. There wasn't anything you couldn't get at the bottom. This would be my informal education on maneuvering the prison underworld.

Paz and I linked up with Boston, Stan, and Eric. Boston, was on his way to the crib so he was pretty much clean. Eric had his hands in everything—numbers, loan shark, bookie, block canteens (the black market commissary in each dorm), card games, and anything else he could get his hands in. Stan was an old head. He kept money in his account so he didn't worry about a hustle. He just shot pool and would blind you with his quick release on the basketball court. Paz, he sold cigarettes and had a card game. We all kicked around at the bottom for a while talking about the streets, who we knew, where we hung out, who we ran across on state amongst other things.

After the yard closed, Paz and I walked back up the hill. He told me that he was a teacher's assistant in carpentry, how Mr. Taylor was a cool guy, and that I needed to find a trade to take when school started back. It was June of 2003 and school started in August, so I had time to figure it out. What perplexed me was I wasn't sure what trade I wanted to do first. I went to the dorm and pondered on the direction of my future and waited on chow.

I got tired of eating cheese sandwiches for lunch. Since I was a vegetarian I just asked for the substitute when I went to the chow hall, which was more often than not two slices of cheese and two slices of bread. After enduring the cheese diet long enough, I decided to get on a special diet which was (vegan) just to get a proper meal. I wasn't necessarily vegan by definition. I was a vegetarian and have been since 1999. I ate cheese and eggs; however, I didn't drink milk.

Being on the vegan-special diet, I met quite a few interesting people from different houses of thought. The first guy was my man "Ty" from Greensboro by way of Norfolk, Virginia. Ty was a practicing 5 percenter, so we did a lot of "building" (discussing cultural topics). At this point in my life, I was a practicing Rastafarian and I'm on my way to be well-versed in that aspect. We built on the similarities and differences within our respected communities. We talked about our desire to get this free bachelor's degree and take advantage of the rest of the free trades that were offered. Ty was a slick talker and could talk himself into or out of anything. He was so good I wondered how in the hell I even met the man. Like I'm sure if he had one more minute with the judge he would have let Ty walk himself out of the courtroom with the judges' apology for his inconvenience.

After long contemplation I finally decided that I would take carpentry. I chose this trade for a number of reasons. First, there was a long list of trade courses, but because Paz was the teacher's aide, I stood a better chance of getting in. Second, Stan was taking it as well. Third, I saw some of the work that the students produced and was amazed. So it was etched in stone. Carpentry would be my first diploma.

Mail call came and I was expecting a couple of letters from some of my lady friends and family members alike. I was standing close enough to the officer that he had to reach around me to hand other people their mail. He finally called my name, but gave me no envelope, only a sheet of paper folded and stapled to keep it closed.

If I had drank any water, it would have turned into steam. I couldn't imagine what was in between the folds. I opened the paper and the letter stated that I didn't score high enough on the reading comprehension on my GED. Therefore, I needed to take a placement test prior to being eligible to enroll in a trade. My blood pressure probably went through the roof because not knowing where I stood academically put me into a panic.

For the rest of the day, I confined myself to my bunk. I always give myself one day to wallow in my sorrow. The next day, I began to search for solutions. Walking around the camp, I bumped into Ty and told him about my dilemma. He told me he received the same letter. I was searching the yard when the answer was in my block. I was sure Rah-Born could help me navigate this problem.

I finally got to the block and found him. I handed him the paper that had me distraught. He read it, and chuckled, and handed it back to me. "Man come with me," he said.

I trailed him into the dayroom, and there he pointed to the bookshelf. "Okay," I said with my brow arched.

What he said next was the hand that tightened the light bulb. "You said that you want to go to school, but first you must know how to learn and seek information." He opened the bookshelf and thumbed through the books until he found a GED book and pushed it into my hands. "Go to the language arts section and work the problems."

I had come to him with a problem and left with a solution and confidence. I hit the yard to go to the canteen and get some snacks. I came up with the plan of studying while everyone was on the yard and at night while everyone was sleeping. It would ensure I had peace and quiet to focus.

I went through two different language arts books within two weeks. I studied these more as a way to build my confidence than for learning purposes. Once I built up my confidence, I was anxious; however, I patiently waited for the placement test. My date finally arrived and I was called to the testing area. I felt a little intimidated after finding out that the test was given on a computer. Just as I walked in, I was told to pick any computer that was on and have a seat. About five more people arrived, and then Mr. Davis gave directions on how to set the computer up for the English version of the test.

He told us it was not a timed test, so we should take our time. That was music to my ears. He also said we could go back and change our answers if we got stuck on any problems, which had been my biggest fear since we were working on a computer. I hadn't thought it would be possible to review my answers. After about a minute of deep breathing, I read my first passage. There were a total of fifteen passages and I took my precious time to read and reread each one. After completing the test, the computer gave me my percentage and I was thrilled to receive such quick results. I had passed and I was on the road to getting my first diploma.

While waiting for school to start, I began working out with Paz to kill time. I started with no expectations at all. I didn't want to become one of the stereotypical muscle-bound inmates. Therefore, I didn't lift heavy; I used moderate weight. Over a period of time, Ty would come to get me so that we could run in the mornings. We ran, at a minimum, twice a week. With running and working out, I imagined I was in good shape, not to mention that I was a vegetarian.

During our workout sessions, I noticed how many people would stop Paz in the middle of a set to buy roll-ups. Sometimes it became a distraction because it would mess up the flow that we had going on, then the individual would want to hold a conversation about some other nonsense, like how they didn't get any playing time in the intramurals basketball game that day because the coach was tripping, or how their number got "jacked off" because Shaq made a free throw at the end of the quarter. Once we got back to working out, our muscles had cooled off or we would be so far out of sync that we would end up walking laps around the yard.

One particular day, I found myself asking Paz about the cigarette business during one of our walks. He broke it down to how he got someone to roll up his Top's tobacco into about 42 cigarettes a pack. He sold each one for five cents apiece and twenty-five cents for a Newport. He said that he was about to stop selling Newports because he was tired of dealing with certain people. He also said that it kept a little money in his pocket. I asked him if it would be cool to get a couple of boxes of Tops to sell. He gave me the nod so I got on my grind. From that point on you could never catch me without roll-ups and Newports.

One day while walking laps around the yard just trying to get my thoughts together, I began to think of all that I'd encountered over the past three and a half years. I knew I would see far more in the next nine and a half years than I had since my first day in the county jail. With this acknowledged I said that I would begin to keep a journal to document the rest of my experience. In this journal, I vowed to keep my innermost thoughts, poems and note my journey.

I've always known that I could write far better than I could hold a conversation because I had a second chance to make it right on paper. From time to time, I would cash in on my writing abilities by writing letters for those who were not so good at putting words together, like giving a woman verbal gratification. Then I would write for those who just couldn't. Either way, I think that I got the most gratification out of it because I got a chance to put my thoughts and feelings on paper and get a response back, although it wasn't for me. While writing letters for individuals, I also got to learn about their strengths, weaknesses, and insecurities.

A guy who was on my block, saw me in action one night, sitting at the table with a thesaurus, dictionary, and a big cup of coffee. I'm not big on making small talk when I'm writing because my thoughts are flowing and one-syllable uttered will throw off my rhythm, so I ignored his presence until I completed my final thought.

"What's good, rap?" I asked with a hint of agitation.

"Yo. I heard that you have a mean pen game. What do you charge to write letters," he asked.

"I usually charge like a box of roll-ups, but if you want me to write a poem and a letter, I need a pack of Newports." So I began to write letters to his girlfriend as well as to his mother. Among him being one of my biggest clients for writing letters, he was also a big consumer of my roll-ups. So in writing letters to his mother, he would often ask for her to send him some money in his account and someone else's too. Not to mention that his mother was the legal guardian of his kids so this kind of bothered me a little. One day while he and I were leaving the chow hall he bought a roll-up and told me that he was about to quit smoking. I laughed it off in a sarcastic chuckle. Don't get me wrong, I really wanted him to quit because it was a struggle for him and he made it a struggle for his mother as well.

"Udy, I bet you twenty dollars I quit by next week".

"Homie I'm not sure if that's a wise bet for you. Nah I'm not going to take food out of your kid's mouth over no shit like that!" I knew deep down that he could if he wanted to; however, his desire to quit wasn't as great as his desire to please his urge for nicotine.

"Don't tell me that you are scared of money or losing your money, as many roll-ups that you sell. Shit. You can get that on your Newports alone in one day." I thought about the situation. Maybe all he needed was a little challenge for him to stop.

"You know what? I'll take your money, 'cause I know that you can't stop." By selling cigarettes, I knew basically all of the other guys who did the same. Knowing everyone in that circle was beneficial. The bet was on, and my man was doing great until I saw him coming around the corner blowing out smoke one day.

"You caught me!" he said when he saw me.

"Damn right I caught you! Now I want my money!" I didn't even have to use my resources to find out if he was smoking. I saw it with my own two eyes. Damn, I really wanted him to quit, because I didn't want it to come to this.

Learning to Learn

This was a moral dilemma for me because I knew physically he could not beat me. I didn't want to take food out of his kid's mouth either, but I couldn't let the bet go unpaid. If I did, from that point on, I would be a sucker and no one would pay me for my cigarettes. So I let the situation linger for a while. Apparently, my job as his letter writer was gone because weeks had passed since I caught him smoking and I hadn't written anything for him since then. Our communication started to taper off, until I finally asked him about paying me.

"Give me your name and opus number and I will have my mother send you the money to your account." He said it so leisurely.

I could not and still can't to this day wrap my mind around that mentality. But once again I believe in doing right by others. So I said, "Just pay me in installments."

Wednesday was the day that we received our weekly draw. This was like income taxes on the camp, and boy did the money flow! Because the guy was in the same block as me, I figured he would want to take care of me first, since I gave him a break on paying me the whole thing. Once again, was I wrong; he looked at me as if we were good. I didn't question him because I knew he had money on the yard, so I'd wait to say something.

Around this time the "Jaycees" (which was like the Masons of the penitentiary) was pre-selling orders of Papa John's Pizza for the Super Bowl. Paz and I went in half with each other and I wanted to buy my own as well. I waited until we got into the block and asked the guy who owed me money if he forget about me. Before I knew it, I raised my voice. This was definitely a battle I wasn't looking for because I knew he wasn't capable of handling a twenty-two-year-old bull, full of frustration. I walked away to put my shoes back on just in case things got out of hand. No sooner than I got to my bunk, I felt a fist to the back of my head. I was stunned, yet reacted off of reflex. I turned around, grabbed him, and slammed him as I'd seen on WWE so many times. The back of his head and my eye both hit the wall locker. The both of us were knocked unconscious, when I came back to my senses, I was on top. I thanked the Most High for that favor and then pounded his face repeatedly. The next thing I knew, we were in the hole for ten days.

While in the hole. I tried to nurse my eye because it is swollen shut. There was no way I could read, write, or go outside. I thought, and listened to music and the guys talking through the vent. From the first day that I got to the hole, I heard a familiar voice. I never acknowledged it because my head was throbbing. At one point, however, it became unavoidable.

I hollered, "Omar Webb, is that you?"

He responded jubilantly, "Udy? I know damn well that ain't you!"

"O, what in the hell are you doing in the hole in Harnett? I heard that you were at Brown Creek." I said.

"I am; I just got caught up in some bullshit down there and the hole is overcrowded right now."

I heard O tell his homeboy how we first met on the youth spread. When O first arrived at Polk, I helped him with his mattress cover across the yard, and from that point on he and I were cool. We talked and caught up on each other's lives, how much time we had left, and what we planned on doing with it.

Super Bowl Sunday came and I was in the hole. This makes the second Super Bowl that I've ever missed, and both since I'd been incarcerated. I'll never forget the New England Patriots versus the Carolina Panthers. We listened to it play by play and you could only get a signal if you were in the right room. If not, you missed it. You just had to listen to the regular radio stations and hope that they kept you updated. It was just my bum luck. I was in one of the poor signal rooms with a black eye and Janet Jackson exposed her breast during the halftime show!

Fresh out of the hole, my eye had healed up just in time. I was ready to go back to school. That was if Mr. Taylor let me back in. After I got my bunk assignment, I dropped my things off and put everything in my locker. I immediately headed to the school gate waiting to hear my fate.

Had I missed too many days of school or not? I needed to get back in so my plan could work. I still had Paz as my inside man and I felt as though I made a good impression on Mr. Taylor and the principal of the school. Waiting patiently on Mr. Taylor to arrive, I laughed and joked with other students over the fight and the situation as a whole.

"So Bullock, they tell me you got the snot beat out of ya. Ain't no sense in me throwing you out of school too," I heard a country drawl say, coming from the window.

It was Mr. Taylor. He came outside and told me to come back tomorrow with the rest of the class. I made it back to class and begin to put my all into learning about wood and reading blueprints, because if push came to shove I could get into the construction field and do carpentry. Throughout the school year, I learned quite a bit and enjoyed the process of getting a blueprint, ordering my supplies, and then seeing it all come together.

By the end of the class, I had made a nightstand, gun racks, cubby holes for kids, and the most exclusive, a podium that Paz and I made together. The guy was a genius when it came to carpentry. He could look at a picture and then reproduce what he saw. I really got a kick out of learning to use different tools and making things with my hands. Although I wasn't so skillful using the scroll saw, Mr. Taylor gave me the job of creating nameplates for the case managers and other staff members.

I was taught how to write the name on the wood and cut it out by one of the teacher's aids. This guy made it look so simple. When I sat down and attempted to follow his moves it was as if the blade had grown dull all of a sudden. The blade wouldn't cut anything but my fingers. It made me feel super incompetent. After I thought I had gotten the hang of it, I showed Mr. Taylor a couple of my finished products.

He laughed and said, "Hell Bullock, you'll use all my damn sandpaper trying to straighten that out."

I chuckled a little but was upset. I responded, "As much as I cut myself and still haven't gotten it right, I don't think I'm the man for this job."

He laughed and agreed and took me off that assignment. For the rest of the day, I walked aimlessly around until I saw Paz and Stan struggling to fit some things into the spray booth. I knew this would be my opportunity to finally learn how to spray paint. I took it upon myself to find a place and assist until I got the opportunity to spray. Once we finished setting up the spray booth it was time to leave for the day. Outside, I talked to Paz and see if he would make a call for me to get on the project with him. He agreed and just like that, it was done.

When I got on the yard, I saw Ty. He asked me if I had seen the guys who had just shipped in. I told him I hadn't and asked if there was anyone I need to see. He said there was a slim guy who had some super locks and was looking for a Rasta to kick it with. Ty and I walked the yard for a while and talked about the reggae artists Sizzla, Beres Hammond, and Buju Banton. When we reached the top of the shoot, I see a slim guy walking with a little bounce in his step, but what stood out about him was the crown that he wore on his head. The crown was huge and filled out, which meant that his locks were wicked.

I said, "Blessed Breddren."

He returned the greeting, and I reached out my hand to shake his. He introduced himself as Mouse.

I told him that I was from Wilson and he said, "Yo, Kaya was telling me about you."

That was all the validation I needed and I'm sure the feeling was mutual. The three of us walked around the yard and talked for the remainder of time the yard was open. I told Mouse that I would get with him the next light (the rising of the new sun), and then I had to go to school. Once I got out, we could link up. From that day forward, Mouse and I would be like each other's shadow.

A little after Mouse's arrival, we stood at the bottom, after chow. In the midst of our conversation and me selling roll-ups,

156

Mouse's facial expression changed. His eyes locked in on something or someone. With his head turned away from me, he said. "I know that light-skinned Breddren with the locks from Foothills."

"Well, call him over."

As he approached us, he said, "Blessed Breddren."

He introduced himself as Atibo Tafari. Mouse didn't have time to tell me that Atibo was Ras, but it was so pleasing to have another Breddren on the yard with us. The Trinity! We talked for a while, then we walked him to medical for his orientations visit.

Atibo said that at the camp that he just left he had to start the Rastafarian service, so this became the mission of the Trinity. For the next couple of days, we wrote individual letters and then combined the strong points; we sent letters to different members of the administration and the chaplain. Weeks passed and we received no letters or responses from anyone. We walked into the administration office unannounced and demanded to speak to the superintendent who we were told wasn't in. Neither was the assistant superintendent. Once we left a message and our names, we walked down to the chaplain's office. When we walked in, the chaplain was putting out the new daily bread pamphlets. I could tell he was startled by our entrance by the way of his jerky motion when he saw us.

"How may I help you guys today?"

"We are here on the behalf of the Rastafarian community. We are just following up on our letter that was not responded to by you or any other member of the administration," Atibo followed up with his quick barrage of questions.

"You should be receiving a letter very soon from myself and the administration. I am setting up for Bible study tonight, so I will have to reschedule a meeting with you guys."

I kind of saw that he was a little uncomfortable with this scenario and tried to brush us off to buy more time. Mouse and I looked at each other, and I nodded my head.

"So are there five circles of five chairs," I asked and his face looked as if I had put a flaming torch under a thermometer. "If so we can do it and place the Bibles in the seats if you'd like." Since I wasn't big on talking and Mouse was somewhat of a hothead, we tried to open the door for Atibo to get him in the office with him.

He saw our countermove and shot a counter of his own. "I'm about to step out and will call you all back down so we can discuss this matter and to help with the setup."

We all looked at each other and chuckled as we saw the chaplain fish through his pockets for his keys and make a motion toward the door. We exited the building with no more rebuttals. We had just been check-mated. It was cool because we learned how to play political chess with him from that day.

We put our heads together and began to use our resources. We knew that there was an administration janitor and the chaplain had an assistant. We understood that most people had a price to do things that we couldn't do ourselves. We paid each guy to slide letters wherever and whenever we needed. We wrote to the Division of Prisons in Raleigh to tell them about our plight and ask for advice on the proper way to get it done.

During this whole ordeal, I graduated from carpentry and started the business associate's degree program. I was also taking an independent studies course in sociology, so my brain was all over the place.

We had meetings on what our next move would be, who would write the next letter, and to whom it would be written. After roughly eight months of repetitive lies and reasons why they couldn't accommodate our request, the three of us were called to the administration office to speak with the assistant superintendent. She said that she had received calls from Raleigh and wanted to get a visual of the guys who were complaining about being discriminated against because of their religion. She said that she was tired of receiving letters and phone calls about this matter. Therefore, she was going to allot us time once she could get the chaplain on the phone. He eventually came in and found the most awkward day and time for us to meet—Wednesdays from 2:30 to 3:30. We had to leave class early and sometimes almost miss chow, but our task was to just get in the door and attend, and then we could change the time in the future.

My first semester of college was incredibly challenging, to say the least. I could not wrap my head around the whole school thing. Studying, reading textbooks, and writing papers were kicking me in the ass with a black steel-toe state boot.

The math was foreign, and the vernacular was above my head, so I began to question my intelligence. I thought I had read enough to prepare myself. I was on the verge of dropping the whole idea of getting a degree. I figured if I got dirty urine, I would be kicked out without looking like a quitter, so I started smoking weed on the regular.

One day, I talked a fellow student into smoking with me before going to class, which was the easiest classes we had; we always loafed off. When the guy stood up to go to the restroom, he fell into the door and was knocked out. I could not express the amount of fear that seeped into my soul. As the officers cleared the room, I stole a look at him lying on the floor and panic began to take over me. My high had been long gone. Once we got outside, a guy from our study group called me.

"Udy, what the fuck did ya'll smoke?"

He saw the concern written on my face, so he tried to calm me down. I chuckled but was mentally out of it until I saw the guy walking out of the building with the medical staff and an officer. Once he was good, we were called back into the class. I wasn't there for the remainder of that day. When we were dismissed for the day, I went to medical and checked on him. One lady asked me to leave and told me it was not my concern. I made eye contact with the cool nurse, and she looked at the door, so I left.

I stood in front of the building and talked to one of the medical janitors. He hadn't gone in yet, so he couldn't give me any feedback. Once he went in, the cool nurse came out to smoke a cigarette. She called me over and told me that he was ok, but was a little dehydrated. She said she liked it when the guys looked out for each other. She said that he would be in there for a while because he was on an I.V. When he was released from medical, I walked him to his dorm. He said that his smoking career was over, and his focus was on school and getting home.

When the progress report came out, I was doing good in everything except

math. The teacher called me into his office one day and told me, if I studied and worked a little harder I could pass. However, if I continued to move as I was, I would fail for sure. I told him that I studied with a couple of guys. He asked how much time I spent studying alone. I thought and I could honestly say not too many. When I left his office, I walked to my dorm and grabbed my radio. I walked my normal running route to brainstorm and create some structure for studying.

I played out a normal day for me. I came up with the idea of coming in straight from dinner and taking a nap from 7:30 to 11 p.m. I didn't have an alarm clock, so I would either find someone who stayed up until 11 to wake me up and I would leave a wake-up note on the officer's desk if they were cool. It was surprising to see how many officers took pleasure in waking me up to read and study. Once I got into a routine, my teacher saw a change in my grades. He pulled me to the side and asked me what had changed. I told him how I had set a study schedule and why I chose the time when not too many people were awake. He congratulated me and told me to keep up the good work. I still had a big hole to dig myself out of, but I had found the challenge to be interesting, so I accepted it and no longer wanted to quit. I wanted to figure this shit out. I wanted to make my family proud of me and I wanted to see it through for personal fulfillment too. I made it through the first semester and started to get the hang of everything.

While fighting to get a better understanding of school, my sister Nic-Nic came to visit me. I was looking forward to a visit. I really needed to see someone I loved. When I saw them, I lit up like the North Star.

We took pictures, and the boys and I talked about school and sports. I asked about our parents, and her face took on sullen expression. She dropped her head and when she looked up she had tears in her eyes.

She said that our father was still doing about the same. He would go to the hospital from time to time for his diabetes. I was aware of his regular visits for his diabetes, unless things were getting worse and no one had told me. I asked her how Ma was taking it being that she had to go to work and take care of him. She said that Ma was good. She said that Da had to start going to the hospital every other day to start his dialysis treatments.

I tried to console her and let her know that he would be alright. Deep in my gut, I worried about the progression of his sickness. We continued on through our visit and tried to keep it all smiles. She began to brighten up when we spoke of our sister Ronnie and her kids, and them coming home soon from the Navy. As we started getting deeper into that conversation, the officer announced that visitation was over. On my way back to my dorm, I pondered my father's situation and accepted it. One thing I knew was I could not hold on to "out there in here." It may sound a little harsh but everyone that tried to live on both sides of the fence were always emotional or mentally unstable. I put it in its little compartment and did my time.

When class was officially over for spring break, I planned on going hard on the weight pile and getting my minutes up running. I even played a little more basketball. One day while playing a full-court game, I was going up for a rebound and somewhere in mid-air my lip caught an elbow, head, or some other body part that caused it to pour blood immediately.

I was in luck. I was playing on the court right in front of the medical station. When I went in, they gave me a towel and told me I might need stitches even before looking at the cut. The camp's doctor wasn't in that day. If I needed stitches I would have to be transported to the local emergency room. I didn't think that I needed stiches, but if the nurse said I did, then I did. It meant I'd have to take a ride off the camp. Before I could be transported they had to clear the move with the administration and get me shackled and handcuffed. I painted a pretty scenario of feeling a sense of freedom on my trip to the emergency room. The shackles, chains, and the two armed officers crushed my dream ride. My mind recalled all that I'd read about the chattel part of slavery, being moved in chains to and fro. It was similar to a walk of shame.

When we reached the hospital, I was put in a wheelchair to prevent me from falling. There is one guard pushing me in the chair and the other walking with my medical chart. The doctor is ready to see me upon my arrival. I guess their fear of any mishaps taking place from dealing with a "dangerous criminal" kind of help speed up the waiting process. The doctor took one look at my lip and begin to laugh. He looked in my medical jacket and said I might need a tetanus shot more than I needed stitches.

"Who's working in medical today," the doctor asked the guards. The guard answered, and the doctor said, "That sounds about right. Go figure!"

I ended up getting a shot, some triple antibiotic ointment, and a trip that I wish I hadn't taken. A couple of days later my lip was healed all the way up, and I was ready to play basketball again. I woke up early the next morning and began to stretch and loosen up. Just as soon as the announcement came over the intercom that all the yards were open, I grabbed my water and Walkman, then hit the yard wide open.

I walked to the yard that I liked to do my running. I walked about two laps and then started my journey. When I ran I was free. I had some good music to assist me with my exodus. When I felt pain, I would always say, "The price of freedom is sometimes pain."

I told myself this to keep my feet moving and to keep my mind from wandering from my current freedom. And just as quick as the pain began, it was subdued by this mantra. After my run, I turned down the volume on my Walkman, grabbed my water, and walked the same track to cool down. I then headed to the block to steal a shower. We were only allowed one five-minute shower a day and it was to be within the allotted time 4 to 10 p.m. I would turn the water on in the shower and duck down so the officers could not see me. When you steal a shower, it has to be done in record time so no move was wasted. In and out.

My inventory had grown quite a bit with my cigarettes. I knew a lot of people through my business. I always sought out new ways to gain a little extra money. Most of everyone that I sold cigarettes to played numbers also, so I could be a one-stop shop. The numbers that I ran were off of the basketball games, either NBA or college.

In the NBA you had four chances to win and in college only two. The way that your number came out was at the end of each quarter, you would take the last digit from each team's score and that was your number. If at the end of the first quarter, the Hornets has 38 and the Bucks has 25, the number was 58, for example. Each number was sold for at least 50 cents. Your return would be five dollars if you hit.

I started off kind of slow because I was new to the numbers game. It's one thing to sell cigarettes, but it's a whole different thing to have people trust you with their money if they hit. As I began to be known as a paymaster, all my numbers became contracted out so all I had to do was go and pick up my money for the numbers on game night. I found myself buying a lot more numbers from other number-men since I started running myself.

My numbers were 01 and 89. This combination was easy to find, so I made it my business to put at least $5 on each number. Every now and then, someone would run a $5 board which would pay out $50. If you hit that big board along with all of the other numbers that you had contracted, you would be well off for a while.

As always, I walked around the yard to find the guys who I had played with to pay for my numbers. When I got to Troy, he said that he is running the $5 board, since it hasn't been run in a while. I played out of obligation. He always played on my boards and bought cigarettes from me. After playing all of my numbers, my pockets were so light, I had to touch some of my cigarette money. At that point, I realized I had gone overboard with my gambling. The game wasn't a game anymore; it was a burden.

I had just enough money to get a meal for the night to look at the game. The first quarter—01 came out. I was to the good then. I began to count my money in my head. Third quarter—01 again. Oh, I was straight. I had well over $250 and really didn't have anything to do with it but put it up.

I walked the yard the next day with my chest out. I looked out for my homeboys and bought myself a pair of shoes. I thought of new ways to get this money working for me, which lead me upon another adventure, loaning money. Who could I loan money to though?

I wanted to be careful not to loan too much out at one time and get beat. I figured that most of the card players would need loans from time to time, so I put the word in that circle that I would do 50 cents on a dollar while other guys did 75 cents on a dollar. I still sold cigarettes and played a few numbers but not as many as I had been. I just wanted to keep money flowing, so I didn't have to ask for anything from home.

As the second semester began, there were rumors of the camp doing away with cash. And just like every other rumor, there was a little truth in it. When the official word hit, we were given a two-week notice; we had to turn all of our money in to have it put into our accounts. Of course, I could not turn in all of my money, so I put some in other people's accounts. Back to the card again, and stamps being the currency.

Soon after the cash was taken, our visitors were given a form to be filled out. A photo copy of the adults ID had to be mailed in with the visitation form, in order to be approved. Then on top of that, your family had to call in to schedule a visit. I knew that this would drop my visitation drastically. None of my homeboys was going to do that; some had charges and wouldn't risk their freedom to come see me, which I understood whole-heartedly. With the cash gone and the whole dynamics of the camp changing, I began to regain focus on school and speaking at the Rasta service. With this focus, I managed to graduate from Central Carolina Community College (C.C.C.C) with an associate's degree in business administration. Both of my parents came for this graduation. We ate, took pictures, and talked. It was really a beautiful moment. I began to see sincere smiles on their faces. It made me happy to make them happy. I had gotten a real degree. That was the first goal accomplished.

I took on my next goal only because the timing made sense and it would definitely make my journey a little easier to travel. I contemplated long and hard on whether to enroll in the Shaw program and finish the last two years of my bachelor's degree. I calculated the remaining time of my sentence and compared it with how long it would take me to finish Shaw. I had a little over six years left on my bid. The case manager could only bring you up for minimum custody once you reach sixty months. Once I completed Shaw, I would be pass the sixty-month mark. With all of my schooling, I should get minimum custody with no problem. That was one of the hardest decisions I was forced to make in a long time. Looking back, it was fairly elementary.

When enrollment took place I was at the head of the line. I wanted to get it out of the way. My mind raced with all the opportunities that would come with a bachelor's degree. I knew that it would nullify the felony that I had on my record and balance out my life. Weeks later, we all received acceptance letters and reality set in. I sent my letter to my mother because I wanted to bring that smile to her face once again.

The difference in taking classes at Shaw and taking classes at C.C.C.C was that Shaw had night classes. It meant Shaw students had to either take a trade or work during the day. I decided to take Electrical Service Technology (E.S.T). This course consisted of breaking down computers and building one from scratch, a slight form of programming, and trying to stay awake. The teacher was either narcoleptic or bored himself as much as he bored us. The only thing I can remember that pertained to the class was Boolean Algebra. That's the way circuits are simplified. I have no idea where to begin if you were to show it to me right now. I do know that I did enjoy it once I broke the code of how to do it. My grades were terrible though. I did just enough to keep a "C."

Shaw was a lot easier than I initially thought. We only had one class a night. In my first year, the only classes that challenged me were physical science, ethics, and public speaking. Our physical science teacher was a fast-talking, hot-headed guy who never taught from the book. His notes were the book and he would be quick to say, "Do the damn work and don't worry about a grade. Just get understanding."

I did somehow comprehend that part. You could tell that he had a drinking problem. It was confirmed when he caught a DUI because his face was in the jailbird paper. Somehow this didn't hinder him from coming to class and talking shit.

My ethics teacher was a sweet older lady; however, she made you think and defend your opinion. At the end of every chapter, we had to write a ten-page paper. If you didn't have an opinion on the topic, you had best get one formulated quick and have a way to defend it with facts and not thoughts or feelings.

She told me one day at the end of class, "Ron, I can't figure it out. You write some great papers, but you don't seem to produce the same during our discussions."

I was well aware of this. I got nervous in the middle of class—having to voice my thoughts aloud. She assured me that all I had to do was not think so hard and let it flow. It really helped me to know that she knew my situation. I tried to engage in the daily topics but always found myself getting lost in my own thoughts. I just fell back to using my energy to put it all on paper.

The public speaking class was a nightmare with the thought of standing up and speaking in front of my peers. The teacher was an older guy that grew up with my father in the mid-sixties in Wilson. I didn't care if he was my father's best friend, I just couldn't calm my nerves long enough to stand and give an effective speech.

"Bullock, you have to find confidence in what you are saying. If you don't believe your words, no one else will. I don't care how good it may be."

I could tell that he and my ethics teacher had discussed my phobias. I knew it was just me in my own way, but I didn't know how to slide myself to the side to allow growth.

I somehow contracted some type of respiratory infection. The only symptoms I had were that I went to medical for about four months for a dry cough. They gave me cough syrup every visit until I brought it to their attention. The cough that I had needed to be treated with more than cough syrup. I was put on the docket to see the doctor. When the doctor came, he did x-rays and found that my lungs were inflamed. They rushed me to the medical ward of Central Prison. From the time that I arrived until I was cleared a month later, I stayed in a quarantine cell.

I had to be the last to read the newspaper. When anyone came into my cell, we both had to wear a mask, and I had to take a shower late at night. For most of my stay, I slept and read John Grisham's books. I didn't have my card, so I couldn't order anything from the canteen. The kitchen kept messing up my food. I was on the vegan diet and they would send me fish and chicken. When I told the officers, they said okay and I didn't see anyone again until I was given my medication.

I couldn't look in the mirror because there wasn't one to look in. I knew that if I looked like I felt, I looked horrible. After a full month of this torture, I was released to general population until a shipping day and then I went back to Harnett. It's crazy to say but I had never and will never again be so happy to see a prison yard.

When I arrived and put my clothes on, I noticed that I had dropped a good fifteen pounds. My hair was dirty and all I wanted was to take a good bath and wash my locks. Once I got on the yard, the Rasta brothers were waiting for me and helped with my bags. I could barely make it to my dorm. Every step, it seemed like someone stopped me, wanting to talk.

No sooner than I dropped my bags on my assigned bunk, I headed to the school and made sure I hadn't missed too many days. When the principal came out he let me through the gate. We talked about my medical problem, which made me realize I hadn't been formally diagnosed with anything. He made the numbers add up and I was back in school just like that. Now all I had to do was go to my class at Shaw and do the same. I was certainly behind on my work, but the teachers there made it work there as well. After getting adjusted to school and eating again, I found a routine and picked up my weight.

I finally got in the camp and settled in. Doctor's visits became more frequent. I was sent to Chapel Hill to a respiratory specialist and given a total of three inhalers. Out of all of these doctor visits, I still wasn't told or given any type of diagnosis until I went to the specialist. He said that I may have had a form of pneumonia and that was it.

The first time that I got the chance to call home, my mother had news that superseded my whole ordeal. She told me that she had gone to the doctor herself and they found a lump in her breast. She said that they were running the test again. The first ones came back as cancerous. She said she was waiting for a second opinion. When I heard the word "cancer," I said fuck my little issues. I was good. She said she wanted to wait until I had got my health back together to tell me. Nothing in the world could ever prepare me for this type of news. After I hung up the phone, I tried to apply the same principle as I had with my father, but for some reason, the shit wouldn't work. I've always seen my mother as a strong woman. To hear vulnerability in her voice broke my soul.

It took me back to my very first visit in jail, when I saw the pain etched in her brow. I heard it in her voice this time. I had to come up with a game plan on how to deal with this thing. I needed a compartment to put it in. I needed to focus on school so I could see her smile! Just like everything else, I found a place to put it. I needed to build the strength in my lungs, so I started running again.

During my runs would be the only time I was allowed to think about my mother's situation. The more that it hurt, the harder I would push. I started off with ten minutes with my target goal always being forty-five minutes. She no longer wanted to come to see me. She didn't have the strength and she didn't want me to see her in her condition. I told her I understood the not feeling well, but she was my mother and I didn't care about her looks. I loved her and needed to see her. She was still my rock and the reason I strived to do well.

It would be my last year of Shaw. I was so excited to get the ball rolling. There were so many promises and hopes for the near future. Hopefully, after all of these graduations, I would be promoted to minimum custody. I would have less than sixty months when I finished Shaw. I planned it all out as I saw it and wanted it to be. But one thing for sure and two for certain, I had to start it before I could get it over with.

This time I chose brick masonry to be my daytime course. I was never interested in laying any bricks, blocks, or any type of stone. I took the class to stay occupied during the day, and a couple of other Shaw students were in there as well. We could study together, go over homework, and discuss class.

I didn't think that there was so much work to do in masonry. The teacher was a young guy. He was an officer at the prison prior to getting the teacher job. He was pretty cool, a lot cooler than when he was an officer. When he saw that we used his class as a study hall, he got a little harder on us. I learned to lay a brick to the line, how to lay block, and make mortar. I didn't mess with the saw because I had an incident in carpentry when the wood flew off of the table saw and hit me in the thigh. I never messed with a saw again. My nerves would have no part of it.

When I really wanted to get away and think to myself, I would go outside and start laying brick to the line. I wasn't that good, but I found some type of therapy in it when the weather was right. On days like that, I would make an exception to my rule and think of my parents for that brief moment.

Our teacher asked the entire class if any of us wanted to help to lay the brick for the barber school that was being built. I did, but my first day was also my very last day. It's easy to do something to clear your mind and another to do it as work. The guys who were on the project were pros at laying brick. I couldn't make mortar with them let alone lay a brick. After I saw that I couldn't lay brick like I thought, I began to keep them stocked up on bricks and other supplies. When they said that I had to get on the scaffold, I decided then and there that my help was no longer needed. I stayed in the room and did my homework from Shaw or wrote letters, but I would not get on a scaffold. The class was a breeze and it was an easy diploma. I did learn a lot but, it just wasn't my cup of tea.

I don't think I'd ever been so anxious. In my mind, I was already in minimum custody. I talked about it all the time, but I hadn't even been given my first assignment, let alone turn one in and I'm rushing the process. I knew that this would be no cakewalk, so I fought to regain my thoughts.

I participated in every activity that I could to help the time go by. I tried to find myself something to do at all times, from school to sports. I played softball and soccer during the weekdays and basketball on the weekend. I ran when I found the time, but I never sat still for a minute other than doing homework.

School proved to be not too challenging. We had the ethics teacher again for part two, the public speaking teacher was our English teacher, and a class called quantitative methods. I had no earthly idea what that was about. It didn't help that the teacher showed up, dropped our work off, and left only to return to pick up that assignment and drop off another one. We had to really put our heads together and gain some type of understanding of this course. I guess his idea was that we wanted to be given something for nothing so he just gave us work and made us earn it.

The year went by smooth. I gave a little bit but not too much. I was going to graduate. My task now was to get my mom to come because the graduation ceremony would be on her birthday. I was given three tickets for the ceremony, so I invited my parents and my paternal grandmother. With graduation so close, I decided to do nothing but go to school, the chow hall, and the dorm. This way I would avoid any trouble.

Graduation day was May 27th, 2008. She was still going through her cancer treatments on her birthday, but my graduation was a day she wouldn't miss. I had no idea that my family came until I actually walked into the graduation hall, which was held at the chapel. I was like the third or fourth in line, so I sat in the front row and had to stand until all of the other graduates came in. During the standing, I got a chance to make eye contact with my parents. They smiled smiles that warmed my heart, the kind that made me stick to the task.

The program was over before it had even started. There were no long speakers and I was thankful for that. When we turned our tassels, my mom cried, and I felt accomplished. We walked out of the chapel and once everyone was outside we congratulated each other. It had been a long ride, but this was only the beginning for some of us. Another chapter needed to be taken on before we could close the book.

Now that I had my bachelor's degree, I could focus on getting promoted to minimum custody and prepare for my release. The "bid" was over. It was time to begin to mentally prepare myself for getting out, freedom, my exodus, the real world… But it all began with getting minimum custody.

During this wait, I got a dorm janitor job. It didn't pay much and wasn't something that I really wanted to do. I needed to stay on gain time and be active. My task was to clean the dayroom and bunk area twice a day. Sometimes it really amazed me just how foul and nasty a grown-ass man could be and walk around with the audacity to want someone to respect him. I would find all kinds of filthiness in the dayroom. It was never uncommon to find wads of tissue on the top of a locker. Sometimes the tissue would be filled with mucus, others with semen. It all depended on who the locker belonged to. I never reached anywhere I could not see. I never touched anyone's personal belongings, and never touched their beds. I didn't want anyone to claim that they were missing anything, and you never knew what a guy did in his bunk.

By having the dorm janitor job you really get a sense of how institutionalized guys are. Some people would pay me each week just to have their chairs and table where they like to sit in the dayroom. I didn't give a damn about sitting arrangements. I just sat in an open spot or sat in the back, wrote letters, and read a book.

One day while setting up the dayroom to everyone's wishes, I was called to the mental health building. I was startled and nervous at the same time. Why was I being called to the mental health building? What the hell had I done? Was my mother alright? Was my father alright?

As I walked past the officer desk, the female officer pulled me to the side and said, "This is the beginning of the process. Take your time and read it good."

I said, "Okay, but what are you talking about?"

"Oh, you didn't know that you were on your way to take the psych test?"

"No. It never crossed my mind. Okay. Now it all makes sense," I said as I headed toward the door.

I picked up my pace. I didn't want to stop and talk to anyone along the way. I sped up to a light jog. When I reached the door, I beat two swift knocks and stood with a pounding heart. When I entered the room, I saw four others waiting as patiently as they could. Some picking their nails, others playing with pencils or buttons, anything they could get their hands on to calm their nerves.

The test was said to have been for violent offenders to see if they would be a threat to the public. It was usually taken prior to getting minimum custody. Once I took my seat, I began to twiddle my fingers. The psychologist stood up and began to go over the instructions and gave us an hour and a half to finish. That was far too much time for one hundred questions. I did the test twice to double-check my answers, then I turned it in and left.

I had a custody review coming up in a month. This gave me high hopes, so I went straight to see my case manager to see what the chances were of me getting promoted on my first shot. When I knocked on the door she motioned for me to come in. I waited to be asked to be seated, but what she said confused me.

"I've been meaning to get in contact with you. You have a pending assault charge, and your case has been sent over to Mr. White."

Shit. After that blow I was caught off guard and speechless. "How long has Mr. White had my case now?"

"For a couple of days, you may exit now."

Now my brain was in overdrive. I could not let this take me off of my game plan. As I began to walk the yard, everyone was a blur and their voices seemed muffled. All I could hear was my thoughts. Just write to the clerk of court in Wilson and get them to check to see what I had pending and go see Mr. White, I told myself

On my way to see Mr. White, I ran into Atibo. I started telling him my problem and he burst out laughing. I looked at him with the most confused face I could produce.

"Shit. You call them problems? I say you got some good problems." I couldn't wrap my mind around what he had just said. He continued, "Breddren, you are about to get your honor grade. They just taking you through the loops right now. Shit.

I still got two more years before I'll even be eligible. Come on. Let's go see this damn man."

The more we walked the more he chuckled at my situation. When I got to Mr. White's office, it was like he was waiting for me because he was coming toward the door as I approached. He opened the door and I entered.

"Ms. Stevenson told me that you may be on the way down here," he said.

The conversation was long because I think I asked the same unanswered question at least ten times. Long story short, he had doubts if I would get my minimum custody on the first shot; however, he did say that wasn't official. That was enough for me to cling on too.

That weekend Nic-Nic and my twin nephews came to see me. When I went into the visitation hall the officer came to me and said that he had to get on one of my nephews for sagging his pants. I told him that I would talk to him about it during our visit. My sister had come to give me my update of what was going on with our parents. Before she even began, I talked to my nephew about his pants and gave him a quick history lesson on sagging. He showed me his belt and said that they were just big pants, to which I agreed.

My sister gave me a brief run down. For the most part, nothing major had changed, and everything was good. The boys told me about school and how hard middle school was.

They said they were going to go trick-or-treating the following week, with no masks. We laughed and joked for the most part of the visit. I told them about my current dilemma. I had already written the clerk of court, so I was just waiting on the response. She assured me that it would play out in my favor.

After all of the visitors were gone, the other inmates and I waited in the visitation hall to be called to be searched. While I was waiting, the same officer approached me again, restating what he had said earlier.

"The next time he comes in with no belt on I will not let him in."

I stood up and with every inch of my soul, I said, "Fuck you. If your stupid ass was really looking he had on a belt and you would have seen that the pants were just big. Keep fucking with my people, racist ass pig. I'll show you something."

His face turned beet red, he grabbed his cuffs, and stood there pondering his next move just as I was. I knew I couldn't fight him, so I conceded, held my hands out, and said, "Now lock me up, you silly ass racist."

He walked toward me with his cuffs extended and put them on extra tight. He walked me to the lieutenant's office. She asked me what had just happened. I explained to her every detail, and I repeated every single word that I had said. I was sent to the hole and was denied my minimum custody.

After going through the whole ordeal of trying to play the game of getting my minimum custody I was on the verge of going back into "bid mode." I started playing sports again, soccer, softball, and basketball. The weather was breaking, and my second shot was soon coming. I was called to Mr. White's office out of the blue.

When I got there, he told me he may have some good news for me this time. He told me that my points had dropped since I just had a birthday and it had been six months since my last infraction. At that point, I had less than four years left. He said that he would bring me up in May. Time had been dragging. Everyone was leaving, and I was practically on a different camp at this point. I played sports to pass time. My mind wouldn't allow me to read and even my writing had slowed down.

The wait had intensified with only the vibration of his words. I slowly backed away from doing anything again. One day I called home to check on my parents, and my father had just been rushed to the hospital. After getting all of the information from my nephew that he knew, I hung up and walked to the clothes house to change my weekly clothes. Ol Skool told me that my name just came up as being minimum custody. I was wondering why things always came in twofold. Could I just get some good news without there being some bad news lurking?

I rushed out of there and found Atibo and told him about my new situation. We laughed together this time. When I called back to check on my father, they let him go home. His sugar level had just been too high.

I quickly put in a transfer request to go to Orange Correctional as my first option and Greene County as my second option. Weeks later I called to tell my parents I would be leaving soon. My mom said that my father was put in the intensive care unit the day before. Damn. This shit was happening too fast. She was working on a year of being cancer-free and now my father's health is growing worse.

I wrote a letter that same night to see if they could switch my second to my option. I needed to go to Greene County to be closer to my family. I explained my situation in a detailed manner. I didn't get a response. No one had really officially told me that I had minimum custody. I just saw it on the roster log beside my name. I tried not to call home too much because I didn't need them to worry about me.

While talking to Atibo in the hallway of the dorm, a guy who I no longer dealt with came to me and said, "I know we don't see eye to eye, but I just wanted to let you know that you are shipping out in the morning. You are going to Orange."

We shook hands and talked briefly, and then he walked away. Atibo and I looked at each other dumbfounded, and then we embraced. It had been a long ride. We vowed to link up on another journey.

To double-check his words we walked to the library to see if I could check out a book. Camps was funny about their books, so they wouldn't allow you to check out a book if you were shipping out. When we get in there, I look around and found a Langston Hughes book of poems. When I reach the desk they looked in the computer and said that I had a book out already and I had to turn in that one first. I didn't make a fuss, because I knew I didn't have one out because I wasn't reading at that time.

We walked the yard and I found the people that I really dealt with and told them my next move. After we did that, the yard was closing, so were the pages in this chapter of my bid. Once the yards were closed and the phones were turned off for the day, an officer came and asked me how many shipping bags I needed. This was music to my ears.

I looked forward to reaching my destination, yet I wasn't happy about going through the shipping process—waking up early in the morning, eating a half-cooked breakfast, waiting on the shipping bus to come to pick us up, then going to Sandy Ridge, waiting there, getting on another bus then riding to the next destination. As I went through all of my personal belongings, I threw away everything that had little or no value.

I gave away anything that someone else wanted if I didn't want it.

Once the packing was done, I sat in the dayroom and pondered the opportunities that the near future would bring. I thought of my father and his situation and how there was always some good and not so good well blended. I played back the past six years on the camp in my head and how I achieved everything that I had set out to. Looking back, I would say that I felt very accomplished.

I sat in the dayroom drinking coffee and listened to an older Cuban guy tell me about his life and his mistakes and how we don't get any replays in life. He told me I needed to take advantage of my situation because he and his son wouldn't ever get that chance. He left me with, "….some jewels I could sell if I chose." When the officer came, I told him I would hold it down and remain focused. This chapter was closed and amazingly effective in the building of me as a man.

Chapter 6

PLANNING TO LIVE

s the bus pulled up to the front gate, I stood and stretched. I couldn't wait to get the hell off that cramped bus. I didn't know exactly what to expect in its entirety; however, I did know that this would be different than anything that I had been accustomed to for the past nine years.

My name was called for me to get off the bus, I repeated the normal routine of reciting my name and opus number to the officer before getting off the bus. I found my personal belongings and waited for the rest of the guys to line up, so we could go through the processing procedure. The officer looked at me with my browns and chuckled.

"You are in another land now, buddy. Go in that building," he said as he pointed to the building straight ahead of us, which looked like it was built in the '50s. "Stop at the desk and tell the officer that you are a new transfer, and he will get you some greens."

I strutted up the slight hill with three white bags of my most prized possessions. Once I entered the building, I was escorted to the dayroom, the officer searched my belongings and patted me down. Once I put my belongings back into my bags, I was given my dorm and bunk assignment, and then directed to the clothes house.

When I reached the clothes house, I was finally rewarded with my first pair of green clothes. I threw those damn brown pants in the trash with force and the entire clothes house staff laughed. I told them that I had just spent nine years in browns. To some that was small change to others, that was a lot of time.

A bald-headed, slim guy with a big beard asked me which camp I was coming from. I said Harnett, and he and the other guy said that they were there once. I looked at the bigger light-skinned guy and recognized him once he said something. He cut his locks off since the last time that I'd seen him. They called him J.P. Now it all came back to me. Once we both recognized each other, I think that we both played our last encounter in our heads and chuckled. That's why it's always important to be mindful of who you offend.

My last encounter with J.P took place on the basketball court. We played one-on-one for a dollar a game and I couldn't beat him because he was wiser and stronger than I was. I got upset and threw the ball over the fence and walked off. My homeboy Paz watched the game and saw how everything played out, so Paz paid him for me. I end up paying Paz back and apologizing to J.P. He accepted it but refused to deal with me from that point on. Once we chuckled, he congratulated me on getting my minimum custody. He said he hoped that I had calmed down since then, and I assured him I had. I told them my dorm and they pointed me in the right direction. In my head, I was glad that we were both mature and handled that with a laugh.

Once I finally got all of my clothes and linens, I headed out to find my dorm. I kind of gave the camp a small look over once I walked outside. It was definitely nowhere near a thousand people here. As I rounded the corner to head to my dorm, I was stopped by a random guy and asked what camp I had just come from.

When I responded, he said "Man, you are right at home then."

He began to run down the names of everyone that was there from Harnett. I knew a lot of them very well. He tells me that most of the guys have either gone to work or gone out on a pass. I got tired of holding all of my personal belongings, so

I thanked him for his information and headed off to make my bunk and chill for a while.

Just as I walked off from the guy. I saw Rah Born wearing street clothes and walking through the gate. Once he was patted down and we locked eyes, I dropped my bags and we dapped and hugged. He asked me where my dorm was. I pointed to it and he told me that he had to go to the sergeant's office. He said he would come down and help me get my things together after.

When I entered the dorm I was amazed as to how empty the dorm and dayrooms were. There were a handful of people in the dorm, but not enough in comparison to the number of bunks. I looked around for an officer but found none. I was so used to seeing a guard everywhere I went at all of my previous camps. As I began to put my things in my locker, I heard Rah Born coming through the door in the dayroom.

"How in the hell did you get out of the damn gate? Boy, you got these people fooled," I said in a joking manner. We both laughed and shook hands again. He helped me get my bunk situated, and then he wanted to walk around and catch me up on what was going on in the camp and with himself. I never got a chance to ask, but he knew that I had observed that there was a lack of visible officers. He always tried to be a big brother to me. I found it hilarious how he felt the need to put me on game or whatever he thought was important.

After walking around the camp for about an hour, guys began to get off work from the road squads, town jobs, and work-release jobs. As the guys started to come in the gate, we took a seat on the benches in front of the office under the shade. Rah Born seemed to know everyone since he had been there for three years already, not to mention that he was a big talker. On one of our laps, I was telling him about my diet and asked him if they would honor it being that the camp was little. He took me to the chow hall to talk to the kitchen manager, and he directed me to the chaplain.

Rah Born showed me where I needed to go and told me to find him once I finished talking to the chaplain. When I knocked on the door, a Mr. Rodgers-lookalike answered the door. He invited me in, introduced himself as Chaplain Earl, and then he offered me a seat. Before I sat down, I extended my hand and introduced myself. He accepted the gesture and sat down at his cluttered and worn desk. His office was very tight and looked like a hoarder's space. He seemed to be better than most of the chaplains that I'd seen.

"So Mr. Bullock, how may I help you?" he asked me.

I told him "I just shipped in today and needed to switch to the vegan diet." He then began to ask questions about my life and how my sentence had been going. I told him that my father was in the hospital and in I.C.U. We talked about my father's health issues and how long he has been in the hospital.

After we talked for a while, he offered to give the hospital a call for me.

He got through to the hospital, but the receptionist told him that patients in I.C.U could not accept phone calls. He told me what was said and told me if there was anything that he could do for me just to let him know. I assured him that I would and thanked him for the help and his show of concern for my father's condition.

When I left, it was getting late and the camp was busy. It seemed like all the guys were in from their work-release jobs. I ran into one of the coolest older guys I've met on state, Doug B. This guy was a self-taught computer genius. I've always looked up to this guy for having done so much time and being able to cope with it so well. He built computer programs throughout the prison system, from small programs to help brick masons add up their materials to the most intricate programs for some of the institution factories. Not to mention, he was first incarcerated when the only computers were in government buildings, schools, or the homes of the wealthy.

After talking to Doug, I felt inspired and ready to get the ball rolling. When I got to the dorm, it was count time and an eventful day. As I sat on my bunk, I introduced myself to at least half of the dorm by introducing myself to my bunkmate. Everyone else interjected and asked questions about other guys they knew and people that I may have known. It was cool, but

I'm no big talker, so I'd phase myself out of the conversation, and left them talking among themselves.

Count cleared, and it was chow time. When I hit the yard, I linked up with three guys from Harnett, we walked to the chow hall, sat, ate, and talked until the chow hall closed. We found a table on the yard and caught up on time. Rah Born was walking around looking for me and found the four of us already at the table talking. Rah Born brought lively energy and we laughed until the yard closed. We walked to our dorms; they probably talked about what tomorrow held for them and the truth is I honestly had no clue. I did know that I had reached the ideal location for progress. I just needed to know how to capitalize on the whole situation. I had almost four years to put it all together.

Weeks went by and I began to see what I wanted to do. I really wanted to go out on the road squad. Just to get off the camp and explore my newfound half-freedom. I told Rah Born what I planned to do and the reasons why because he always wanted to know if there was any logic in the next move.

We talked and walked the yard, he stopped mid-stride and said, "Hell, naw man. Don't get away from what you've been doing."

He began to walk away, but at that point, I was lost. "How the hell you going to walk away like you dropped a jewel to let it linger."

He said, "When I first met you, you analyzed the camp before you started dealing with them dudes, the same shit applies here. I know that shit look sweet, but it's a lot of snakes on this little ass yard, and you gotta sit back and figure out who is who, 'cause I can't tell you every single one."

"That shit makes a lot of sense, but what the fuck am I supposed to do. I haven't cut hair in over six years, and I don't want to work anywhere else!"

"I'm not saying that you gotta cut hair, but try cook school and get a chance to see these dudes in action. Once you see it you will thank me."

I took heed because he had three years on this camp and I knew it was something that he had seen before. The following day I wrote a letter to my case manager and the cook school teacher to apply for the class. There was still a class going on at the time but it was in its last weeks. When my case manager got my letter, she called me to her office. I had no idea what she wanted with me, but she hadn't talked to me since my second day. When she opened the door she was holding a folder with name on it.

I waited to speak and for her to make her way around the desk, and sit, before I sat down. I was kind of thrown off when I saw this. She opened it up, began to read some things off, and then started asking questions about my plans for the remainder of my sentence. She asked me about my infractions, but showed interest in my last one.

She was concerned that I somehow slipped through the cracks because the infraction was less than a year old. She said my points dropped just enough to get into minimum custody range. I could definitely explain thoroughly.

My birthday came around just in time for some points to drop by two. My custody review was every May and November. I couldn't understand what the problem was. She said that I would be on some type of probationary period, so if I got into any type of trouble I would be sent back to medium custody. I couldn't wrap my mind around that because I had met all of the requirements.

I asked if she would recommend me for the cook school. She agreed and told me that it would probably help me to stay out of trouble. I caught write-ups from time to time, but that wasn't on the regular. Prior to my last infraction, for cursing out the guard, I hadn't been written-up in two years. That was for cursing out a guard, but that was it.

That conversation rubbed me the wrong way. It was the Friday before Memorial Day, so the camp was full of energy. The case manager along with the men's club was putting on a cookout for the entire camp, so there was a lot of moving going on in the program's office. Guys from the men's club were loading the office with cakes, sodas, and chips. After leaving her office I put my headphones on and walked the yard, thinking how hard I had worked to get to this point and they wanted to contest if my being here was legit. As I walked I began to just let it go. Shit. I'm here now! What was meant to be, will be.

Monday rolled around and the chow hall was shut down after breakfast. There was a lot of movement on the yard with the men's club and the case managers getting prepared for the cookout. Most businesses were shut down so there was no one going out for work-release and the passes were minimal. With the camp having the majority of the guys on the yard it was easy to get a couple of good games of basketball.

I found Rah Born and we checked the games out with some of the other guys we knew. While we were all together, I told them of my situation. They assured me that it was hard to get into trouble unless you were just a hothead. They expounded more, but I was still a little worried because at the end of the day, the administration could do whatever they wanted to and be justified by each other.

I dropped the topic and watched basketball games. The type of games that I used to see at the medium and close custody camps was totally different in temperature. The screens and picks set were legal and done with less force, the fouls were not as violent. The difference was that most of the guys who were playing had a lot to lose. Some had work-release jobs and others just had community passes. That was enough to keep their temperament calm and cool.

What shocked me was that the yard closed with only two more points to go. The officer walked around and told them that they could finish the game and they would count us on the yard once they counted the dorms. This was something I never experienced so I had to stay and finish looking at the game. Once the officers came back to count us, the game was done and we were all sitting on the benches, so there wasn't much for the officers to do. Soon after the count was cleared, and the case managers called each dorm individually to go to the outside visitation area to get your food. They opened the chow hall up there would be enough room for everyone to eat.

When I reached the visitation area, I spotted Rah Born and we sat together. He joked about switching a real hamburger for my veggie burger. Once they were finished serving everyone, they called for seconds and I doubled back to grab some baked beans and potato salad. Before I made it back to my seat, the sergeant called me to the office.

I was kind of nervous because I was still playing the scenario in my mind from what the case manager told me. I didn't know if they were going to ship me back to medium custody. That was the longest sixty feet I've walked in a very long time. When I opened the door, I stood in the waiting area until an officer peeped through the door and waved for me to come in.

When I entered the sergeant's office, I was prepared for the bad news because there was a somber vibe in the room. He sat at the computer and looked up at me with a caring face. He looked as if he hated to deliver the message.

"Mr. Bullock, your sister just called and told me to inform you that your father passed. I can call her for you if you would like me to."

I was speechless. All I could do was just shake my head. He called my mother's number and I spoke to my mom and sister. They were shaken up and all they wanted to do was make sure that I was good. I was. There wasn't anything I could do other than accept it, and crying wouldn't do anything.

After I hung up the phone, I thanked the sergeant and walked back out to the table and continued to eat my food. My thoughts were with my mother and far away from Orange Correctional Center. When I sat down, Rah Born asked me if everything was alright with the family. I told him that my dad had just died. I moved on to what we were talking about prior to me getting up and getting my seconds. I honestly had mixed emotions about the whole thing. I knew that my dad was very sick, and the way that my family described it he was suffering, so it was selfish for anyone to wish him to be present and continue to suffer.

The following days were a blur. I received letters from people I hadn't heard from in years. The guys on the camp passed a card around and everyone signed it. My Breddren, Atibo, got the guys at Harnett to sign a card to send me. Atibo also called my mom, and my homeboy, Snott, sent me a card. Shit like that meant the world to me. They were guys that I built with from the yard, they were on other camps and made it their business to send love during a loss.

Following up to the funeral, my family made arrangements for me to go home to be with my family for the funeral. The day of the funeral was surreal. When I got up, I showered and then called home to speak with the family. I was kind of excited and nervous at the same time. It had been so long since I had been to Wilson. What was I to expect? Who would I see? And how would it be to see the family that I hadn't seen in ages?

As I laid back on my bunk and contemplated my day, I heard my name called over the intercom to report to the office. I headed out, ready for the ride and experience that I had ahead of me. When I made it to the car, the driver was Officer Riley. Officer Riley was a brown-skinned, short, pudgy guy with salt and pepper hair. We talked the entire ride there and he asked me a million questions. When we arrived in Wilson, my mom had left the transportation payment at my grandmother's house with my Aunt, so he took me there. While I was there, I put on the suit my family left there for me. I was given enough time to put on my clothes and talk to the family members at the house.

Once I finished talking to my family, I told Officer Riley that I was ready to go to church, which was right around the corner. We reached the church, he told me that he would sit in the back; I was free to mingle. I tightened up my hair, took a deep breath, and then walked to the front of the church and looked in the casket.

I couldn't recall the very last time that I had seen my father, but I knew that he looked so at peace. I stood there as if we were having a conversation, I heard a voice that I had known from years past.

"Hey."

I turned around and replied, "Hi, how are you doing?"

It was Ms. Boo-Boo, Ms. Cymp, and Isha. Ms. Boo-Boo said, "Give me a hug, looking like your daddy."

I gave each one of them a hug and did a little small talk. After they walked to their seats, a couple of other people came up and talked to me, none who I really knew. I heard someone say that the family cars just pulled up, so I headed outside to see my family. I think that I floated down the aisle.

As I passed over the threshold to outside, the family cars stopped. I don't know if I jumped down all the stairs or walked down that fast, but I got to the bottom very quickly. The cars just sat there for a while with the doors closed, so I stood there looking through the window waiting for my mother and sisters to get out. My mom opened her door first then the others were opened. I held the door open and closed it behind her and we just stood there and hugged for what seemed like forever. Next, I hugged my sisters and the rest of the family.

We lined up as we would walk in and be seated. We sat and listened to the proceedings of the service. It wasn't a sad nor a long service. After we walked out, I ran into everyone I could possibly think of and even ones I couldn't think of from my past. I exchanged information with some who had no intention of using it and others who sincerely meant well, but I still wouldn't hear from them.

I bumped into Isha, her mom, and her aunt again. This time Isha and I exchanged addresses. And then it was time to go to the graveyard. I road with the officer across the street to the graveyard. The officer said that he would sit in the car until I was done. My mom didn't want to re-open the casket, so the funeral home had me seal it and give my mother the key. I hugged family, friends, and took pictures with my sisters before I walked to the restroom in the cemetery to take my suit off and gave it to my cousin. I walked back to the car and prepared for my ride back to prison.

In the next couple of weeks, I just waited for cook school to start, just to get a normal schedule. For the majority of my time, I had a job or went to school. The downtime began to wear on me. I wasn't mentally ready to start working out, I was tired of reading and writing at that point. I walked the yard aimlessly or helped the guys out in the clothes house, just to kill some time. I randomly decided to go to the barbershop to get a shapeup and get my face tightened up. When I approached the barbershop, there was someone in the chair and someone waiting. I heard the TV and people talking next door to the shop, so I looked through the door and saw there was an older white couple holding some type of class.

I wasn't sure what type of class, so I decided not to go in until the lady came to the door and invited me in. They were watching a movie on the civil rights movement. I sat down and watched the remainder of the documentary. Once it went off, the lady introduced herself as Mary and the man himself as Gabe. I then introduced myself to the class; we began to discuss the documentary. The class was awesome; they said the class was called "reading and discussion" and it was held every Tuesday at 1:30.

From that day forward I tried to go as often as I could. Mary and Gabe had some interesting backgrounds and were a very caring couple. Their topics ranged from politics, race relations, and general world issues. I found myself really intrigued by their class and took notes, but, very seldom did I speak. I think they found my quietness interesting. Everyone in the class had an opinion on whatever the topic was while I listened. Sometimes they would ask me questions just to see my response or ask me to stay after class and help them clean up. When I did they would ask me my thoughts on certain topics and we would laugh and joke.

Dealing with them really helped change my perspective of dealing with white people. For most of my life, I've never dealt with older white people on such a personal level other than my teachers in school and my lawyer. Gabe was a community volunteer sponsor so he could take the guys with levels out on community passes. They've been going to the camp for years, so they had built a rapport with quite a few guys. I asked around and they had some astounding reviews on the camp. So, my comfort level really grew with them.

Cook school started and I was glad now to find some normality on the new camp. The teacher's name was Ms. Gould; she was deeply passionate about cooking and teaching her class. She was direct, and she'd let you know her thoughts, so there was no guessing how she felt. My first day was too serious to be a cooking class. We were given a syllabus and told about the papers that we would have to write during the course of the three-month class. I was kind of use to this since I went to college at the previous camp. This was a bit overwhelming to some of the older guys, as it had been ages since they had attended any type of class. I helped some of the guys fill out the necessary papers. The number of grown men who didn't know their social security number was shocking.

The next day we were issued some cook pants, a jacket, and a cap. I thought that was real cool instead of wearing the kitchen whites. When I told her that I was a vegetarian, she was excited because, she had some recipes that she wanted to try out.

The class was broken down into two sections, group "A" and group "B." Each team picked what they wanted to cook each week. In the first two weeks, we just did book work. Learning the measuring cups, the cuts of meats, and the difference between fruits and vegetables, all of the basics. Our first week cooking, we cooked breakfast, the following week lunch, and the third dinner. Everyone on each team had the opportunity to be every position in the kitchen—from the head chef to the dishwasher and server. Each team critiqued overall service and performance of the other. There would always be that one asshole on each team who wanted to call the manager from the other team out and complain about something small.

The competition was serious and quite unbelievable, to say the least. It finally made sense why Rah Born recommended me to take cook school first. Some guys were petty just to be petty. Ms. Gould's cook class was known all throughout the town of Hillsboro; she volunteered to cook for small events on and off the camp. One of the best experiences that she provided was a mock job interview.

She came up with a job title and the entire class had to apply for it. We had to write a resume and cover letter. Then she had three ladies from the community college come in and give us all individual interviews. I was nervous as if this was a real interview. My hands wouldn't stop sweating and my mind wouldn't stop thinking. I had been incarcerated since I was 18 and I was a barber, so I never went through an interview process. I think that I forgot my name during the process, I cussed, and I was chewing gum. To say the least I didn't get the mock job. I think that one of the ladies felt bad for me because once the whole thing was over and we were all back in class, she talked to me and gave me some pointers to ease my anxiety. Upon our completion of the class, Ms. Gould seemed to get the top cooks some type of work-release job cooking if they met the requirements to get a work-release job. She wanted to help the sincere guys advance and I think that was why she was so direct with people. Her bluntness seemed to drive away the cons.

Those three months flew by, I had three more months before I could come up for my level two. I decided to stay on the inside of the camp and try to get the barber job as soon as a position came open. I enjoyed cook school; it was a great experience, and it helped me to see that I needed to work alone.

About a week after I finished school, Rah Born went home. It was a good thing to see him go home—he definitely served his time. The first chance that I got, I went to see my case manager to put a request in to get the next barber job that came open. She said that she had been checking on me through Ms. Gould and the other members of the administration, and I had been given good reviews. She congratulated me for completing school and told me that she would put me at top of the list for the next open barber job.

I let the guys on the yard and both of the barbers know that I was trying to get the barber job when it comes open. The camp usually kept a black and white barber in the shop to make sure there was some diversity. The black barber was a guy from Greensboro who shaped me up so, we were pretty cool. When I told him that I wanted to get in the shop he said that he was about to go home in a couple of weeks. A week after our conversation he shipped out to a camp closer to his home town. And just like that, I was in the barbershop.

I began to get nervous, I hadn't cut hair in well over six years and I knew that I had lost my skills. I could talk a good game, but I knew I wasn't familiar with the clippers anymore. The only thing that eased my thoughts was that I cut at Pasquotank and Albemarle. I knew that it would take me a couple of cuts to get it together. All I really needed was about one full week and I would find my rhythm.

I lied to myself when I said that I wasn't taking any more classes. School had become part my structure and my way of doing time. I couldn't deny myself the opportunity to attain free education. Two of the three classes that I took were incredibly unique and interesting.

One was an African American studies summer course that was taught by two doctoral candidates from Duke University. In this class, we studied the civil rights era, the music, literature, speeches, different groups, and the laws. The teachers had the community, churches, and faculty from Duke to donate books and other learning material for our classes.

I wrote a poem titled "Literature of History" in which I used the titles of books written by black people to tell a story. I'm no big poet so it's not saying much, but that poem by far was one of the best that I've ever constructed.

My next class was a weekly creative writing class. This class was taught or better yet held by an older white lady whose vibe could easily be mistaken for that of a hippie. I enjoyed spending time in this class, everything so structurally free-flowing. We wrote poems, short stories, and all other forms of creative writing. She was an artist in so many forms; she could write, paint, draw, and was a great photographer. Her selection of the music ranged from Jazz, Billie Holiday, Nina Simone, to the Bee Gees, and The Doobie Brothers.

She and her husband were also another couple who helped to change the general view that I had of white people. Once she came for a while she began to bring her husband in to participate in classes with us. He even went as far as to get a sponsor's pass. Not that I was one of the more vocal participants in the class, I guess they like my loud quiet character. Once he got approval, I was the first person that they took out on my first community pass. Once we built a close relationship, they took me to their house. We cooked veggie dishes, drank tea, and talked until it was time for me to go back to the camp.

I continued attending the writing class even when I was switched to the second-shift barber. I would stop in for a few minutes when I couldn't get people to schedule their haircuts around the class time. When I couldn't make it, I would find out the writing assignments and turn them in the following week. When I had any questions in any of the other classes Simone would open up a classroom discussion and we would get to the root of the problem and I would have different perspectives to pull from.

Simone and Dave were heavily into art and Dave was also a disc jockey at a local radio station. I was introduced to art galleries and the radio station in which he worked. The experience of the art galleries was enlightening. I really learned the meaning of "Art is up for personal interpretation."

209

When I saw some pieces, at first, I disregarded the artist's perspective at the time. However, I took into account how it made me feel, or the message I thought the artist was trying to convey. My views have been molded in a different fashion since I experienced the art galleries. I will forever be indebted to this couple for allowing the opportunity to experience the different perspectives in art and life as a whole.

The final class that I took was a political science class. The teacher was also a doctoral candidate, but, he was from the University of North Carolina. This class was interesting, it opened my eyes to the laws and the political process.

I learned that the majority of voters are misinformed and hold fast to the untruths given by the local news. We had to write papers for our test; the teacher said everything except, "I didn't know convicts were as bright as you are.", once he returned our graded papers. He always seemed to be shocked at the level of our discussions.

Upon the completion of this class, we were given a certificate and a couple of credit hours for a college class. President Obama was in office on his first term and trying to pass his health-care bill, so we often talked about the process and all of the things that were attached to the bill. The more I learned, the more ignorant I grew in the political field. If I learned anything, I learned that politics definitely wasn't the area I would focus on. There's always too many moving pieces, to take into account. However, I really enjoyed the class—the topics, the teacher, my fellow classmate's diversity, and just learning about the "system."

By working in the barbershop, I worked in the building next door to the case manager's. In working such close proximity, I had a chance to keep tabs on my custody reviews.

Just my luck when I come up for my Level 2, there was a change in the superintendent and other higher members of the administration. One prison in Greensboro was closing so the staff and some of the population was sent to Orange Correctional Center. During the process, my level promotion was basically denied due to the lack of administration—that's what I was told anyway.

I was hot, mad, upset and any other synonymous that matched frustrated. Getting denied was a setback in my eyes; I had the remainder of my sentence mapped out. I wanted to get a work-release job, work for two years, to have some money to start off my freedom journey with. Not being promoted for level two, forced me to create another game plan. I had to restructure my old plan and keep pushing forward. There wasn't really any other option; it wasn't like I could undo what had been done.

During the new administration, the superintendent brought along with him some of his "do-boys" so the flow of the camp changed. I had never in my entire bid witnessed anything of the sort; a guy name Mark had a direct connection with the superintendent. There was no guard to call him to the office, he just went whenever he wanted to go and talk. I stayed clear of the guy.

One Monday while I cleaned the barbershop I stopped to look out of the door's window. Mark walked by and saw me standing and headed over. "What's up Udy, can I get a quick shape-up?"

"Nah, I don't cut on Monday's. I just clean up and fix my clippers." As soon as I finished my sentence the sergeant called count time. "Come on bruh, you can knock that out while they are counting," he said.

"Nah but I can definitely get you tomorrow." Then an officer walked by and told us to stay in place for count.

"That's cool, I can wait til' tomorrow, where you from Udy?", he asked as he sat down in the waiting chair.

"Wide-A-Wake Wilson and yourself?"

"I'm from Mebane. Let me ask you a question. Why you so standoffish?" "Bruh, I'm at the end of my bid and I like to stay out the way," I responded. "I see you got a select few that you deal with, but if you ever need anything just holla at me." Count was cleared and he extended his hand, I shook it and then he walked out the door.

Mark had guys that rolled with him for whatever they could get out of him and his connections. Some of these guys

I cut their hair so we talked and they gave me the rundown on Mark's relationship with the superintendent, and other officers. The truth was that no one really knew the details of his relationships with any of them, no more than he had actually told them.

One day out of the blue Mark asked me what was my level, when I told him that I didn't have any he said don't worry about it they will give you an early custody review.... Two months later I received a letter from my case manager saying that I had been promoted to Level 2. I asked her no questions; I did pull Mark to the side and ask him what he had done.

He told me that he hadn't done anything but that it was good that I made my Level 2. I walked away scratching my head. Once I started going out on passes and getting a taste of being trusted in the world with no chains, it was mind-blowing. I experienced another side of life that I could have never imagined until I began going out on community passes.

I always wrote to guys I had met along the way who I had respect for. So, Atibo and I stayed in contact since I left Harnett. We stayed in contact with each other through our mothers. I wrote to his mother and he wrote mine. I didn't trust just anyone to leave my mom's address with but Atibo was more like a brother so that was no problem.

In one of his letters he told me that he had just made his minimum custody and he was at a camp from hell. I told him to just stay focused and keep doing what he was doing to stay out of trouble. He wrote me back and said that he was contemplating catching a charge to go back to medium custody. He said that he was at Odom farm which had recently upgraded to a minimum custody camp, but they still ran it like a medium custody camp. He said that this was what they called an observation camp, meaning that everyone had to do at least a ninety-day period before they could go to a normal minimum custody camp. When he told me that he considered going backward my mind began to work overtime.

I needed to help him out of there because he needed to experience what I was seeing. The little bubble in my head popped, I had it figured out. I knew that Atibo could cook and really enjoyed doing it, so I used my resources. I called Mark to the barbershop to get a shape-up, around count time. I gave him my spiel and told him that I needed my brother to get to Orange before he goes crazy. He would be an asset to the camp because he could cook and bake. When I said he could bake, that was the game changer.

Mark said that he would see what he could do and he would let me know something. I wrote to Atibo that same night and told him to just hold on; I had put something in motion for his rescue. I would like to say a good month later after my request, Atibo came in just as Mark had said. I knew the date that he would be coming so I watched the gate and waited on his arrival.

When he got off he looked at me and smiled a big happy ass grin, then said "brother you got to tell me how you made this happen." Then we went on to go through the processing procedure.

I had no idea where he would be housed so I waited outside of the dorm. After about forty-five minutes I went in. Depending on who was working, that act was be prohibited but it didn't matter that day. When I walked in he was on his way out, to go to for the clothes house. I showed him the barbershop first then we walked to the clothes house and I introduced him to everyone who worked in there. Once he was situated, he headed to his dorm and I went to the barbershop. Whenever he finished what he had to do with his personal belongings and making his bed, he too came to the barbershop. When he came in we caught up on what's been going on since we last talked, and then we got to the nitty-gritty. I told him exactly who I talked to, to get him there.

"Shit, I know you don't agree with that shit, neither do I but hell it got you here and closer to home, with a baker's job." He looked at me with wide eyes and mouth dropped.

"You mean to tell me that an inmate got me moved?", he asked.

"Yep, he run the damn camp from the way it looks."

He looked at me and said, "What the hell they got going on around here?"

"I thought shit may as well as get someone else here to witness this shit with me!" we laughed then talked about who was there and what we had going on.

On the anniversary of my father's death, I did a twenty-four-hour fast and cut my locks. That was really the beginning for me. I had to change everything in me and everything about me. I had to be brutally honest with myself. I cut my locks because I needed to change my image. Not only were the locks a change in my physical image but one with an ideal. I mourned the passing of my father in my own little way for the entire year, now it was time to build and start living life and move forward. The renewal process had to start with me, with a little less than two years left, I had to work on me in a major way. I decided to formulate a work-out schedule and stick to it. From that day forward, I put my exodus ahead of everything else. I swore that I would turn into a statue of salt if I was to look back.

After the first-shift barber went home, it took the administration almost a month to hire a new barber. So, for an entire month, I was left to build relationships with all of the people on the camp who got haircuts. And, the barbershop also being synonymous with the psychologist, the barber chair being one and the same with the psychologist's couch. At first,

I didn't see it as anything other than being overworked. But just as I had learned so many other times prior to this one, look at the brighter side of things. This was the side of the coin that I chose to look at from that point on.

Once the new barber was hired, I still cut the hair of the majority at the camp. It paid off as far as getting to know almost all of the camp and my locker overflowing with cakes, cookies, chips, honey buns, granola bars, stamps batteries, and cosmetics. I knew that I had gained a wealth of knowledge in the past couple of months, but I was still getting burnt out in the barbershop. I needed a change of scenery and I had no plans of leaving the camp, so I decided to go to my case manager and see could I transfer to the road squad.

When I told the fellows of my plans to leave the barbershop, nobody was feeling it, but I didn't care. I couldn't focus; I had too much going on in the shop. Not even a week after I told my case manager of my wishes to go to the road squad did she find me a slot open and found a barber to fill my spot.

Prior to getting on the road squad, I had no clue all they did at work other than what I heard them talk about. My first day out on the squad the temperature was right at thirty-six degrees. About six of us loaded into a fifteen-passenger van; the officer driving the van handed me some orange gloves. That was pointless to put on if their duty was to keep my hands warm against the cold. He welcomed me to the squad and the guys showed me how to wrap my bag around a stick to hold it as we walked.

There were two colors of bags—a white one and a blue one. The white was for trash and the blue for recyclables. Since there were only two assigned to the blue bags I was given a white bag.

We road about five miles away from the camp and he pulled off on the side of the highway and put us out. We put up a big sign that said, "inmates working." Shit, reality check. Since my time at Polk I hated that word, so I never used that word "inmate" even before I was lead to the road of self-discovery. I knew I was more than an inmate. In my life, I've been placed in all sorts of boxes, but that's a box I just would not willingly be placed in. I was a part of the system, but, yet, I was not an inmate.

After we put up the sign, it didn't take long to forget about that negative connotation. In less than about half a mile my hands were cold as ice, we walked and talked as the officer in the van drove behind us. I talked and walked as long as I could, but I needed more gloves on my hands and an extra pair of socks on my feet. In mid-stride I turned and began walking toward the van. The guys looked confused and asked me what I was doing; it was cold, and I knew no one really expected us to walk too long in that type of cold for too long.

I stopped the van and got in, they asked me what was wrong, and I told him that my hands were about to fall off, and I needed another pair of gloves. I took off my gloves and put them on the heater and tried to thaw out before I faced the cold again. They saw that I got too comfortable before he said anything. He caught me up with the other guys and gave me an extra pair of gloves, then I got out.

I walked with the other guys when we came off the ramp one group of guys went on the median side and another group took the outside. We were walking with our backs to the traffic that being another thing to think about while walking, "Were the drivers really paying attention while driving"? After walking a couple of miles, the van stopped, and we jumped in, we went back to pick up the road sign and then went on break. As we sat in the van everyone joked on me and made bets of how long I would make it.

I laughed with them, and said "Shit if it stays this cold for the rest of the week I'm done, so make your bets off the weather." Even the officer laughed at that truth because that wasn't even a joke.

The weather eventually broke, and I stayed on the squad and found my spot and became a veteran on that team. We walked sometimes nine miles a day. I used it as the cardio part of my workouts. I was upgraded from a white bag to a blue bag. Being on the squad somehow didn't stop the guys from

219

wanting me to cut their hair, so we worked it out with the barber for me to cut for some of the guys on Friday and Saturdays. The barber began to have health issues; my case manager called me in and asked me would I consider going back to the barbershop. I told her that I would definitely go back. Although I began to like leaving the camp almost every day, I did miss cutting hair. So, after approximately three months on the road squad, I had beat all of the projective quit dates that the guys had for me.

When I got back into the shop, I hadn't lost a beat; I cut all day long. My custody review was nearing, and I would be eligible for my Level 3 after which I could find a real job on the street and could go out with two other people on a pass. That was my main focus at the time.

I had been infraction-free for a little over two years, so I had a good shot. I would keep that to myself because I didn't want the process to be influenced by anyone. I told Atibo when the day came up and that was it. In June, I saw that I had been promoted to a minimum of 3. Now was my shot at really preparing for my release date.

Once it was official that I had my minimum 3, I began to network with everyone who had work-release jobs to see if their employers were hiring at the time. I quickly found out that the work-release thing was politics and it was all in who you knew or how well you knew the individual. I knew quite a few guys very well, and I had two guys put my name into circulation at their jobs. I even had to go out and do an interview with a fabric company. The guy's word that worked at the metal fabrication plant was so strong that I didn't need to do an interview. On his word alone, I was given a work-release job and I was able to make and save money for my exodus.

I was started out on second shift, which was from 1:30 until 7:30 p.m. This time killed all of the day, so it made my time go by so fast. My duties consisted of making sure that all the paint was removed from the aluminum oxygen bottles once they were removed from a huge bin that held hot paint remover. After I made sure they were paint-free, I would box them up and stack them with a small forklift. That was far easier than walking down I-85 picking up trash.

Four months had gone by and I was on my way to reaching 2012. Just as always when things seem to be going just like you need them to, there is always a hiccup in the system. After working on work-release for a little over four months, the company was forced to downsize and layoff three guys on the work-release program. There was however, two guys left from the work-release program and just my luck, the guy who helped me get on out there was still there.

For the first couple of weeks, I would wait on him to get off work to see if anything had changed at the company and each week was the same news, but he tried to keep me hopeful. I soon began to look for new jobs, to no avail. My case manager called me to her office to see if I wanted to go back in the barbershop until I was placed back on work-release. I refused the offer because I was still cutting the guys who I needed to cut on the side. Between cutting hair, working out, and still going to the writing class, my day was full. The only thing is, I wasn't accomplishing any of my financial goals at the time. I really needed to get back on work-release.

One day when I was cutting hair for the guy who got me the work-release job, he told me that the company was looking for someone to work first shift doing something that I had no experience doing, but he would see if they would bring me back. He told me that he would talk to the supervisor and see what was going on and see if he could put my name back in rotation. This time politics had reared its head back into the mix of things.

One of the caseworkers had a guy who she wanted to plug in the open spot, but the company said that they wanted me back since they knew that I was a good worker and no liability to the program. So once again I was back on work-release, this time I was assigned to first shift which was from 6:30 a.m. to 1:30 p.m. It took my body a little time to adjust to the time but once the work began it all began to just flow.

The second time around my duties were basically the same, but I was working with steel instead of aluminum. The paint remover was a lot different, but the principle was the same. Once we got the parts out of the chemicals, we sprayed them off and boxed them up, ready to be sent back to their respective companies. In the winter months it was cold and the summer it was hot; in the non-insulated tin building, we felt the extreme temperatures, we just had to dress accordingly. The work was pretty easy; the hardest part was dealing with the weather.

My work ethic was so good I was often asked to work overtime when they needed extra help. I willingly accepted it with open arms. I needed every red cent that I could get. I didn't know what the future held; however, I did know that I needed money to get where ever I wanted to go.

Finally, 2012 came around and I did everything in my power to learn about any and everything that I thought of or heard was important for me to know when I got out. I read every article in the newspaper, magazine, or leaflet that I felt applied to me and my situation. Isha and I had gotten serious; we had made tentative plans of being a couple when I came home.

My plans were to go home and buy some clippers and get back into the barbershop. I wanted to pick up where I left off. The only difference this time was I needed to get out of Wilson and do it all in another town, city, or even state. I knew that if Isha and I were going to make it, she would need to respect my wishes of not staying in Wilson. It wasn't so much that I was running from anything, but just staying clear of all that I knew existed there.

March soon rolled around, and my anxiety began growing, April 30th was nearing at world-class speed. The majority of the guys who I dealt with on a regular basis had gone home. The pickings were slim. When I walked around the camp, it was as if I didn't know anyone, so it had to be my time to leave.

It didn't seem like it but March had made a year that I had been on work-release, so I was awarded a week of paid vacation time. When I realized that and mapped it out, I pulled my supervisor to the side and told him how I decided to use my time and he assisted me following through with my game plan.

The plan was to use my vacation time the week of the 23rd and get paid on my way out the door. I knew that I would likely ship out that week, so it made sense to me to use that to my advantage. If nothing else had worked out before, this one worked just like a charm.

As I had thought I was on schedule to ship out to Greene County on the week of the 23rd, that Wednesday. When I found out that I was shipping, I went around and kicked it with some of the guys that I really dealt with and wrote down their opus number, so I could write or keep in touch with them once I got home. I went through my things and gave away clothes and everything else that made sense to leave behind. Plus, I wanted to travel light on my last trip.

That night I couldn't sleep, this time I knew I was on my last destination before I went home. I got tired of tossing and turning and my mind racing all over the place, so I just got up and went into the dayroom and made me a cup of coffee and put my thoughts on paper. Before I knew it, the officer came in and got me to go to the chow hall to eat breakfast.

We waited in the chow hall until the bus came. I had the chance to kick it with my former co-workers and other people who were on work-release and had first-shift jobs. Once the bus came, I got on and recalled what an eventful three years I had spent there and hoped that I had learned all I needed to propel me to be a productive citizen. I was finally nearing the end of my sentence, I didn't know if I would end it with a period or an exclamation mark, but I damn sure knew It wouldn't be a question mark.

Chapter 7

EXODUS

When I got on the bus this time, I got off knowing that this would be my very last time on the gray goose. I was walking in a trance. I don't remember any faces or any voices, I just followed the line like a sheep. I followed to the processing room, where we were searched, and our personal property leafed through. Once the officers were done with us, they gave us our dorm and bunk location.

When I walked out on the yard, it was packed around the basketball court. I saw my homeboy talking shit on the sideline, and then I heard my name being called from another area. I could not recognize the voice and couldn't see who it was. I heard it again then I could see it was a slim guy coming from across the court.

As he was calling my name, my homeboy heard it and turned my way, using his hand as a visor from the sun and said: "Udywopp, what's good my nigga".

Now I got both of them walking in my direction, I dropped my bags and took turns giving each one dap. The tall guy turned out to be a young cat I was at Orange with named Rambo, and my homeboy was my lil homie from the Hill named Nut. They helped me take my things to my dorm and set up my bunk.

While setting up my bunk we caught up on what was going on since we last saw each other. Nut told me everyone who was on the camp from Wilson, and honestly, I only knew two of the five. We talked on the regular, but I could not focus on anything that they were talking about or dealing with; mentally, I was already home. I was there and that's it. There was nothing that they could tell me other than how to get my barber license a little quicker.

I had six days left and staying out of the way and getting home was my only objective.

For the next couple of days, I could hardly sleep; that Saturday Isha came to see me. The visit was funny because next Monday I would be going home. She told me how everything would play out, I wouldn't see her Monday because she had to work. But she promised to come through right after work. She dropped my clothes off at the gate, so I would have something to wear home. We did all of the small talk until visitation was over.

Back on the yard to do everything possible to knock my time out. I refused to lift any weights or play basketball. I attempted to read, but my thoughts took over the plot of any book. I tried to write in my journal, but I couldn't think of anything that I had done in the past days that was noteworthy. I walked the yard and caught up on what's been going on in the streets since I've been gone with my homeboys!

They told me of all of the changes with the neighborhoods being divided by gangs, and how all of the older guys were the OGs (leaders). They told me my best bet was to get out of Wilson or to get a package of drugs and hope for the best. Staying there made me cringe but leaving did the same. I had been gone for one hundred and fifty four months, and I longed to be in Wilson and succeed but from the talks of it, Wilson wasn't conducive for any of those things. So, from that point on, my thoughts shifted from going to Wilson to trying to find somewhere I didn't know anyone and succeed there.

That was how my Sunday was spent, just thinking. When it was time to go to bed, my mind traveled from May of 2000 up to April 29th 2012. Sleep was a fleeting illusion, counting sheep, horse, duck, geese, numbers, or anything for that matter didn't help. Somehow I did get a chance to grab some rest from the thin air until the morning. When I woke up, all I could do was smile. I went to breakfast just to get that last meal to etch in my mind what I never wanted to come back to.

I met my homeboys there and we stayed on the yard and walked laps until count time. When I went in for count time, I packed my things and broke down my bed. I was finally ready to make my exodus to society. After the count cleared, I walked outside with my chest poked out. I knew very soon I would hear my name called. I stood court-side and looked at the guys play basketball, and tried to not look as nervous as I really was. In just a few minutes I would be starting the rest of my life.

I was nervous because I had been incarcerated for the entirety of my adult life, I had been told what to expect but in all honesty, I didn't know what to expect. I didn't want to get out and be a recidivist and do this all over again. I was really scared because I questioned whether all the education that I acquired over the past decade would been enough to propel me forward to be successful not just in Wilson but in life in general? While I was lost in my own head, my name was called. But I hadn't finished my thoughts, so I proceed with my rundown of fears and blocked out them.

"Ronald Bullock report to the front gate with your belongings"

I have been waiting to hear these words directed toward me for so long, and when I finally heard them, I neglected to respond.

Nut walked over to me and said: "Udy they called you."

I thought my one last thought before making my great exit. Was the world ready for me? Shit I had just completed 13 years of college! And it was just the beginning.

Made in the USA
Columbia, SC
12 August 2020